JOHN WHITE OF MASHONALAND

DO YOU KNOW

that all the royalties
earned by the sale of
this book will go to
help to cure the children
and grown-up people
of all races in a new
Hospital in Mashonaland
built in memory of John
White ?

JOHN WHITE
OF MASHONALAND

by

C. F. ANDREWS

NEGRO UNIVERSITIES PRESS
NEW YORK

Originally published in 1935
by Hodder & Stoughton, Publishers, London

Reprinted 1969 by
Negro Universities Press
A DIVISION OF GREENWOOD PUBLISHING CORP.
NEW YORK

SBN 8371-2070-5

PRINTED IN UNITED STATES OF AMERICA

Dedicated to

ARTHUR SHEARLY CRIPPS

John's Friend

CONTENTS

CONTENTS

8

FOREWORD

To all who have assisted me in collecting material for this volume, and especially to the Rev. Frank Mussell, of Selukwe, I would return grateful thanks ; and also to Morley Wright and Jack Hoyland, who have corrected the proofs.

R.M.S. *Ranpura,*   C. F. ANDREWS.
   Red Sea,
      Epiphany, 1935.

CHAPTER I : MY HOPE IS IN GOD

" THE one thing," wrote John White, " that keeps me from sheer despair is to know that I am on the path of Providence.

" Surely, if God has called me, I need not tremble. He can qualify the most seemingly unfit. My hope is in God."

These simple words, so characteristic of the writer, were sent to one of John's intimate friends in England from the steamer that carried him out to his pioneer work in Africa.

He was at heart the lowliest of men, without a single thought of self-seeking, full of inner diffidence, always shrinking back with a sense of his own unworthiness ; yet his strong faith in a Divine Providence, over-ruling all things, gave him amazing moral courage and made him fearless in the face of physical danger. For he kept in his soul that " fear of the Lord " which is " the beginning of wisdom." The certainty of being set apart for God's service carried with it an inner consecration, which hallowed the whole of his life.

When, towards its close, a fatal illness laid

him aside in England, far away from Africa,
this supreme trust in his Redeemer became
transformed into a burning charity for all
mankind. The man of action was changed
into the man of prevailing prayer. The hero
in him became the saint.

" God so loved the world " was, in these
days, his favourite text. He lived in the
sunshine of Christ's presence even in the
midst of pain. The upper room, where he
lay, was an inner sanctuary, hallowed by
continual prayer. Those who came to see
him went away with joy and wonder in their
hearts at the power of God's Holy Spirit,
transfiguring human weakness and endowing
it with divine strength.

Yet, withal, he remained a lovably
whimsical saint up to the last, with moods
of fun bubbling over whenever he had the
least respite from pain.

He would even take delight in teasing those
who were with him and would join in the laugh
when his joke was found out at last. He kept
a gay and gallant spirit and rarely complained.

Whenever some old companion of his
pioneering days came to visit him, in Kingsmead Close, his happiness would be touching
to witness. One anecdote would lead to
another, and he would tell his stories, while

he lay in bed propped up with pillows, with that merry twinkle in his eye which endeared him to us all.

Incidents which revealed the kindly nature of his own Mashona people pleased him most of all. He would take immense delight in proving by illustrations their remarkable loyalty to those in whom they trusted ; their power of forgiveness of injuries ; their unfailing cheerfulness and good humour ; their sturdy common sense and practical wisdom. His eyes gleamed with pleasure at each remembrance of them, and it was easy to understand what a rare happiness it must have given to the Mashona to receive him as their guest. For the Africans are simple by nature, and John was simple also.

No one could fight more strenuously on their behalf than John White did. No one, also, could forgive and forget the hard blows more generously than he when the fight was over. He was a true knight-errant for Christ's sake, the champion of the weak against the strong. Very closely he represented the spirit of the poet's prayer when he prays :

Give me the strength never to disown the poor,
Or to bow my knee before insolent might.[1]

[1] Tagore's *Gitanjali*.

There was needed, at that special time in Africa, a prophet, who would stand out against oppression wherever it was to be found and be ready to accept the " prophet's reward." God sent a man whose name was John. If he had not borne witness with a fearless courage in Mashonaland, the whole history of the people of the soil would have been different.

When John lay dying he gave me, after much entreaty, permission to write this book, which should make its special appeal to the younger generation, with the hope that they would carry on his work. At that time I promised in return that before writing it I would visit Mashonaland and meet personally the Mashona about whom the story would be written.

In previous years I had been many times to South Africa and twice to Southern Rhodesia. But on all these earlier occasions I had gone specially to help the Indian settlers and had not been able to see much of African village life. It was necessary, therefore, to make a point of meeting the people of the soil among whom John White had worked. By the help of friends I was able to accomplish this object.

When I reached Bulawayo in July, 1934, I was met by G. H. B. Sketchley, who intro-

duced me to John's friends at that centre.
Then I went on to Selukwe, where Frank
Mussell took charge of my programme.

Arthur Shearly Cripps, the poet missionary,
one of John's closest personal friends, came
to meet me while I was staying at Frank's
house as his guest. There we were able to
have long and intimate talks together while
I went through the records which Frank had
carefully collected.

After this we travelled together through the
Reserves, on to Umvuma and Enkeldoorn, and
from thence to Epworth Farm and Marandellas, reaching Waddilove Institution at last.

Matthew Rusike came with us all the way
to Waddilove and also returned with us, and
we two had many talks together that were
of the deepest interest to me. They showed
me the depth of affection that was in the
heart of the Mashona towards John. I had
other opportunities of meeting the Mashona
Christians. My sympathy went out especially
to the evangelists and teachers—men of
earnest character with a deep love for Christ,
which made them able to endure hardships
and "fight the good fight of faith" with
great courage and perseverance. They need
our sympathy and prayers, for on them, in
God's Providence, lies chiefly the burden of

the work which John White had done so
much to carry forward.

On these and other journeys we had opportunities of meeting those who owed everything that they held dear in life to John's
goodness. It was an unspeakable joy to me
to hear from their own lips their eager witness
and to experience the depth of their love
for him whom they called their Father.

Other friends also I met on other occasions
in South Africa whose devotion to John's
memory left a permanent impression on my
mind. They have given me every help in
preparing the story which follows. In many
ways it is as much their story as mine, for
I owe all the materials to them.

And what a story it is! No one who
reads it can fail to catch the glow of the
ardour of those pioneer days when a continent
was to be won for Christ!

Southern Rhodesia is now a settled country,
traversed by motor roads and railways. It is
possible to go in a few hours a journey which
would have taken days to accomplish with an
ox wagon on trek. A less romantic period has
begun, with new difficulties which have to be
faced. But the spirit of fearless sacrifice
shown by those early pioneers, who first won
the Mashona to Christ, must never be forgotten.

JOHN WHITE was the eldest son in a family of seven children. He was born at Roe Farm, Dearham, in Cumberland, on the border of the Lake District. His birthday was January 6th, 1866, and he was thus sixty-seven years old when he died on August 7th, 1933.

His father, John White, and his mother, Anna, both lived on to a good old age, greatly loved and revered by their children. The Lake District, with all its beauty, was near at hand, and a walk would take those who lived at Roe Farm into some of the most lovely country in the world. The fresh air, blowing in from the sea and over the mountains, made John a sturdy child. He came from a splendidly healthy stock.

A simple, living faith in Christ, as taught in the Wesleyan Communion, hallowed the village home where John was born. His parents were deeply religious Cumberland folk, and an atmosphere of love and devotion surrounded him while he was a child.

Yet, at first, in his younger days, he tended

to drift away from his father's and mother's faith. He was unable to make it his own. But his parents silently commended their first-born son to God and continued instant in prayer that his heart might be given to Christ.

John's early education was of a meagre character. A poor widow, Jane Allen, kept a school, where he learnt a little reading and writing along with arithmetic and other subjects. But even this did not proceed very far, because the young boy had soon to put his schooling aside in order to help his father on the farm. He told me that those days, when he was engaged in farm work, taught him more than all his school lessons put together; for his father had a fund of practical wisdom and became in many ways his teacher as they went about their farm together.

The family moved on later to a larger farm at Stainburn, near Workington, where John assisted his father in a " milk round." This meant getting up very early in order to milk the cows and then carry the milk to the different houses.

During later years, in Rhodesia, this experience on the farm proved invaluable. For it not only gave him a good practical judgment, but also added greatly to his powers of endurance. He had learnt, too, the good habit of making the best use of the early hours of the day.

John White's father was a man of sterling character, respected by all the country-side. For over sixty years, as a local preacher, he proclaimed the Gospel of Christ. Such work was voluntarily undertaken in addition to the duties of a large farm.

John was very fond of telling the story how once, on his return from Rhodesia, he took his father's place in the pulpit in his own village. After the sermon was over the congregation discussed together which preacher they liked best.

" Oh, aie," said one of them, " we like the young 'un fairly well, but we like his father better."

Anna White, John's mother, shared to the full her husband's devoted faith in Christ. She was a woman much given to prayer. John told me that his mother's prayers had done most of all to bring him to Christ. He also explained to me how at first he had no vital interest in religion, though he was always a serious lad at heart. His mind was often troubled when he saw his father's and mother's deep love for Christ and felt his own heart cold. He could not share their experience, however much he longed to do so. Thus he reached the age of sixteen.

Then one Sunday there came to the village church the Rev. John Waugh, a mission preacher. As John listened to his preaching he felt his heart strangely moved. There was a warmth of love he had never known before. Then, while all were kneeling in silent prayer, after the sermon, the preacher asked those who were present to surrender themselves wholly to Christ.

One of the local preachers, who knew him, rose at that moment and went over to him, laying his hand tenderly upon his shoulder as he knelt in prayer.

" Oh, John," he pleaded earnestly, " won't you *now*, at this very moment, make your decision for Christ ? "

That question proved a turning point in John's life. He replied very quietly, " Yes, I will." Then he went out into the inquiry-room and made his life choice. He poured out his heart to God and gave himself wholly to his Saviour with a new passion of adoring love.

John told me how, as he walked home that night, it seemed to him as if the heavens were opened and he was living in a different world. The very stars in the clear night sky appeared to be sharing his joy. For many weeks after he saw everything wherever he went—the mountains, the lakes, the whole country-side—enveloped in a glorious light. It was as if Nature herself was far more beautiful than he had ever realised before. He went long walks among the lonely hills, singing in solitude the praises of God. His natural love for his father and mother and every member of the home grew deeper, and he was ready to take up with joy the lowliest service for Christ's sake.

After this first overwhelming impression had spent part of its force and the thought of the future came upon him, he sought— like St. Paul at the time of his conversion— to find out what the Lord would have him to do. For his whole character was practical. Day-dreaming had no attraction for him. So he gave himself to earnest waiting upon God in prayer.

As the eldest son of a Cumberland farmer, he was naturally a very early riser. After his conversion he began to rise even earlier still, long before the dawn, in order to keep tryst with his Lord, in the silence, before the day's work of carrying round the milk began. Very soon he felt within himself the

divine compulsion to share the good news
in his own heart with others. Each village
in the country district learnt from him at
first hand the story of his changed life, and
many were brought to Christ, sharing his
joy and inward peace. His father and mother
were glad when they saw in him these tokens
of the new birth. They thanked God who
had so wonderfully answered their prayers.

By slow degrees and after much heart-
searching, John came at length to the decision
to offer himself wholly, body, soul and spirit,
to his Lord for the work of the Gospel. His
father and mother both encouraged him to
go forward.

It is noticeable, that from the very first he
seemed to be quite certain that his ministry
would be abroad and not in Great Britain
itself.

While he was in this mood of expectation
and waiting to be told what service would
be required of him, he saw an appeal for
young lay-evangelists, who were needed in
Australia. He was on the point of offering
and would probably have been accepted,
but his superintendent minister prevented
him.

" No, John," he said, " we want you as a
minister, not as a layman."

John was still very young, and took the advice offered with a grateful heart.

Through the kind help of this superintendent he became a candidate for the ministry and was accepted. On being asked at this time whether he would wish to serve at home or abroad, John at once asked to be sent abroad. Yet for some unknown reason —possibly through some oversight—he was at first put down for work at home.

CHAPTER III : DIDSBURY COLLEGE

JOHN was sent to Didsbury College, Manchester, in the year 1888. He found out, after he had been admitted, the mistake that had been made in the register, whereby he had been placed on the roll of those who were to serve in the home ministry of the Church. Therefore he went at once to the Governor, the Rev. Richard Green, and gained his full consent to be entered as a candidate for the ministry of the Church abroad. This immediate acceptance for missionary work gave him the greatest joy, and Didsbury became henceforth his spiritual home.

I can vividly remember the happiness which it gave him at Kingsmead Close, where he lay in his last illness, when I came back from Manchester one evening and told him the story of a visit I had paid to Didsbury—how the whole college was wonderfully responsive and given over to prayer. John's eyes first grew very bright, and then they became dim with tears, as the vision of the past came back to him, when he had been a Didsbury College student nearly half a century ago. It was easy to see, at that moment, the love which he had for the great college in Manchester to which he owed so much. He told me of the wonderful fellowship that existed in his own time between the students and the staff, and also among the students themselves. Life-long friendships were formed and his own dearest friends had been Didsbury men. Perhaps no honour was dearer to him than that which came unasked, when, in his later ministerial years, he was invited on some special occasion to address the students of his old college concerning the missionary vocation. He threw his heart and soul into that address, and it profoundly affected many lives.

John had now obtained his heart's desire. He had been accepted as a candidate for the ministry of the Church of Christ abroad. But where should he go ?

The saintly David Hill came to Didsbury and asked him if he was prepared to work with him in China. John eagerly assented. But just as with Australia, so also with China, this proposal did not advance any further. God was preparing other plans, which were not yet clearly understood. His final work of service was to be in Africa, not in Asia.

The last years of the nineteenth century
had witnessed a rapid opening up of the
interior of Africa. Cecil Rhodes from the
South, for a long time past, had been looking
northward as far as the River Zambesi.
Bechuanaland formed a corridor into this
northern hinterland beyond the Transvaal.
Starting from thence, a column of troopers
and settlers, accompanied by Rhodes's lieu-
tenant, Dr. Jameson, had crossed Matabeleland and penetrated the territory of the
Mashona. Jameson had planted the British
flag at Salisbury and taken possession of the
country as a Protectorate under Chartered
Company rule.

Two Methodist missionaries, the Revs.
O. Watkins and I. Shimmin, had gone forward
from the Transvaal, with a view to start
pioneer work in the north. As a consequence
of this forward move, the Transvaal work
had been left vacant. John was now asked
to take it up, with the hope that he also
might soon be called to the north.

It was at this time that John had to fight
through one of the hardest battles in his
whole spiritual career. For, at the moment
when the call came, his mother was ill.
In her weakness of health her faith and
courage failed. She could not bear to part

with her son and asked him not to leave her.

John said to his college friend, W. H. Whiting, " Pray earnestly for me to-night ! I have heard two voices. One, the voice of my Lord, is asking me to go to Africa. But my mother has written to me saying that she fears it will be death to her if I leave her."

His friend, seeing how distracted he looked, urged him to get a good night's rest, so that his mind might be clear to make a decision on the morrow.

" No," replied John, " I am spending this night with my Lord. He will not fail me, nor forsake me."

Next morning Whiting met his friend, whose face shone with a new radiance.

" It's all right," said John. " You know the text, that he who loves father and mother more than Christ is not worthy of Him. Last night, my Lord assured me that since I am willing to do what He calls me to do, He Himself will look after both mother and me at the same time."

Later on, after the decision had been taken, John had the happiness and comfort of receiving a letter from his mother, asking his forgiveness for having pleaded with him to delay at such a critical moment. Not only, she added, had her own health *not* become worse (as she had feared), but it had greatly improved. When once her mind had been released to obey the will of God, she had rapidly recovered. After this she remained her son's ardent supporter in the mission field to the end of her days.

The Rev. Marshall Hartley gave the ministerial charge at the sacred service of Ordination, when John was ordained. His address to the young candidate seemed to sum up the course of events that followed later. For he rightly inferred that John would remain only for a short space of time in the Transvaal, and then would press forward into the northern hinterland, where a new Mission was being established.

"Let him preserve his health," said the preacher, "so that he may use his body for the service and the glory of God. Let him cultivate deep sympathy for the African races. Let him learn their languages. Let him, like the great Exemplar, Jesus Christ our Lord, be a true man among his fellow-men."

Such prophetic words as these, spoken by one who had himself practised what he preached, did not fall to the ground. They seemed to map out, in a remarkably accurate manner, the course which lay before the young minister, as he thus gave his life into Christ's hands to do with as He would.

John carried these words with him on his voyage to South Africa and kept them often in remembrance. Thus a bond of sympathy and affection was formed between the older and the younger servant of Christ, which proved to be of great value in John's future work.

CHAPTER IV : AMONG THE MASHONA

" I HAVE received a letter from London," John wrote to his friend, " asking me to go north to Mashonaland. It may mean more than I expect. ' Rough ' is hardly the name for the life up there ! Fever is rampant. Wild beasts are plentiful. The Matabele threaten war. Yet I can see God's hand in it all. My confidence is in Him."

Marshall Hartley's prophecy had very quickly proved true. After a short stay in the Transvaal the summons had come to John to trek north.

He had counted the cost long ago ; and when the call reached him, his mind was at rest. " I go there," he continued, " as fearlessly as I would go to my bed. If I never return, I am glad to be counted worthy to die as a free soldier of Jesus Christ."

But a sudden set-back depressed him for a moment. Fighting had already begun and the chairman at home in England ordered delay. Then a second trouble occurred. John's health suddenly and unexpectedly collapsed. The doctor diagnosed nervous

debility, and said it would be suicidal to
go north in such a state. John had over-
worked himself during the first two years
in a new country and had to pay the penalty
for it in a nervous breakdown.

Then followed a gleam of hope. " The
war," he writes, " in the Matabele country
is nearly over ! God willing, it will be a
great joy to me soon to toil there for the
extension of His Kingdom. I long to do
something worthy of the love, wherewith I
have been loved. . . . My one longing is to
be more like Christ."

In spite of this new opening and his own
recovery of health, it was more than four
months before a start could be made. At
làst, on April 30th, 1894, John left Pretoria
for the north. On May 6th the caravan
came to the Limpopo River, where the
Transvaal ends and the northern hinterland
begins.

It took the whole party more than five
hours to get across the Limpopo. It is now
spanned by a great bridge and motor-cars
cross it daily.

They were in " lion country " at last ! On
the second day this became unpleasantly
apparent owing to an accident which John
himself has described.

" We stopped for the night," he writes,
" on the banks of a wide river. Next morning
I walked on, while the drivers were inspanning
the oxen. When I was about a quarter of a
mile away I looked up, hearing a noise. Sure
enough, about two hundred yards away, a
lion was just strolling across the road ; he
walked into the bush. He did not seem to
see me, for which small mercy I was not
unthankful. They rarely attack unless they
are molested, or are hungry."

This was one of the many times when
John met lions in the bush during the course
of his long life in Rhodesia. Often he would
lie down on the open ground to rest, with
the camp fire burning beside him, while lions
prowled round about. Later on, when he
had crossed the great Zambesi River, the
dangers were greater still. But his quiet
confidence in God prevented him from passing
sleepless nights. He rarely had any sense of
fear ; and when any sudden alarm did occur,
giving him a fright, he is brave enough to
tell us about it.

The wild beasts and venomous snakes
which he encountered were by no means the
only dangers. Even before he left the Transvaal to go north he had been caught by the
rapid current in a swollen river and had gone

down twice. He had lost all hope, when a
Dutch friend swam out and helped him back
into the shallow water. The life that meant
so much in after years to the Africans of
Rhodesia was thus nearly lost at the very
outset. But John had committed every
anxiety into the hands of God, his Father,
Who cared for him. While doing what he
knew to be God's will, he took no thought
for the morrow, knowing that his Heavenly
Father kept him day and night in His gracious
keeping.

" One night," he wrote on this first journey,
" I had lain down to sleep, but somehow felt
too cold to do so. About two o'clock I got
up and went to the log fire. Still burning,
it was. I cannot describe my feelings, but
they were slightly weird and sad. Around
there reigned a silence, almost to be felt,
broken only by the occasional shout of a
jackal, or the yelp of a hyena seeking its
prey. The stars shone down in their bright
stillness. I began thinking of home, of
kindred, of friends, of you all.

" Brooding thus by the log fire, I looked
up, and there, just appearing, was the morning star, the bright harbinger of day. Soon
the mules were inspanned, and once more
we pursued our way north.

" Is it not so in life ? Duty calls us from
our dreary musings to the task awaiting us ;
and on we go, until one day, tired, weary,
exhausted, we shall lie down to rest and awake
at the bidding of Him, Who is our Bright and
Morning Star—Jesus Christ, our Lord and
King."

A week or two before their arrival a tragic
incident had occurred to one of a party
travelling on the same road. They had gone
out shooting, and one of their number had
detached himself from the party by accident
and got completely lost. They searched for
him in vain for some days and then were
obliged to go towards the north. They were
delayed, however, by floods at the Lundi
River, and some of them went out again to
shoot game.

To their great surprise they came suddenly
upon a man, half demented and almost naked.
He ran away from them in fright, but they
overtook him. Then they found him to be
their lost companion, who had gone through
such a terrible experience that he had been
brought to the very verge of madness. He
was cared for and nursed back to health, and
became normal once more. But the shock
remained with him all the rest of his life.
It is difficult, while travelling to-day in these

same regions, to realise that things like this happened only forty years ago.

One further incident may be related which illustrates the perils of those early days.

"A fortnight ago," John wrote to his friend Needham, "I had an adventure with a lion, which might have had more serious consequences, had it not been for the good Providence of God. We had walked on for some distance, when we heard a dog bark. He gave two or three more short yelps and then we heard no more. My carriers shouted, but silence reigned. As the grass was getting longer I thought I had better call a halt. So we stopped, lit two big fires, and lay down to sleep.

"At sunrise we were up and away. I was walking first. The tall grass, on either side of us, got thicker and thicker. We had tramped about four miles when suddenly, without any warning, a large lion bounded out of the grass and stood on the path about six yards in front of me. It looked at me, and then, with two more big leaps, it was standing on a boulder about twenty yards away. There it stood looking at us.

"Keeping my eyes on the beast, I walked backwards and got my gun, for I was the opposite of calm. But I thought for a

moment.   The pellets might only annoy him,
and that might have been the end of me.
Taking my rifle, I was about to take aim,
when the beast leapt off the rock and was
soon hidden in the tall grass. We waited
for some time, but it did not appear
again ; for which small mercy I was very
thankful.

" Putting two and two together, I concluded
that this was the beast that must have con-
sumed the dog when we heard the yelp the
night before ; and we had aroused him from
his slumbers after his feast.   Until I met that
lion I thought I was a brave hunter ! "

When John arrived in Salisbury, the head-
quarters of the Chartered Company, he found
a condition of things which disturbed him
far more than any conflict in the bush with
the lions. For in those early days the
administration of justice in Mashonaland was
lax in the extreme.   Everyone seemed to do
that which was right in his own eyes.   Harsh
things were done in dealing with the Africans,
and very little notice was taken of them.
All this came as a great surprise to John,
because he had never thought that such
laxity was possible under British rule.   His
outspoken attitude towards these acts of
injustice at once made him a marked man,

and his mission work in consequence was rendered difficult. But he never swerved from what he felt to be the truth.

A very brief statement may be inserted here to explain the course of events up to the time of his arrival in Mashonaland.

Cecil Rhodes, who had amassed immense wealth from the diamond mines at Kimberley, had obtained by clever manœuvring an agreement handing over all prospecting and mineral rights in Lobengula's territory. This agreement was interpreted as covering, not only the Matabele country, but Mashonaland as well.

Rhodes had formed a Chartered Company and had sent an armed force, accompanied by Doctor Jameson, through the Matabele territory into Mashonaland. This had led to the first Matabele war.

Mashonaland was occupied and administered by the Chartered Company in the name of the British Government. It was a time when the great European powers were still engaged in a scramble for the unoccupied portions of Central Africa, and this new invasion of Mashonaland caused little comment. Ostensibly, it was to protect the unwarlike Mashona against the Matabele warriors.

If the occupation had not been accompanied by new evils, it might have been peaceably made. But the laxity of administration, which I have mentioned, led to excesses on the part of the European invaders. These inflamed a passion of resentment. The witch doctors from Matabeleland adroitly seized the occasion to foment further mischief. In this way, the former hostility of the Mashona towards the Matabele was now turned against the British. Trouble was already brewing, which was at last to break out in a new war.

One day, when John White was purchasing some goods in a store, there came in a tall European, who had already been warned by the magistrate for his ill-treatment of the Africans. The Rev. George Eva, one of the Wesleyan missionaries in Salisbury, had brought his misdeeds to the notice of the authorities, and this had enraged him.

Seeing John White, who was short in stature, the tall man shouted out, " These damned parsons ought to be kicked out of the country ! " Then pointing towards John, he added, " Here is one of them, and I have a damned good mind to take it out of *him*."

John White looked at him with a smile and facing up to him said, " I have heard

big words from the like of you before now ;
but they are nothing more than wind."

The men in the store laughed and the tall
man turned on his heel with an oath and
left the place.

John was obliged at this time to report a
heinous offence committed by a highly-placed
Government official. The case was proved
and the official was dismissed. The friends
of the man were very indignant with John,
but no one dared to lay violent hands on
him.

To come into the midst of such things as
these, and at once take action, gave John
an unwelcome notoriety. But he could not
be true to Christ, his Master, if he remained
silent. Therefore he accepted all the suspicion and disdain that were heaped upon
him as a part of his Lord's service. For
Christ Himself had trodden that pathway
alone and had been rejected by His own
people. "He came unto His own, and His
own received Him not."

A touch of humour, now and then, made
these early days more bearable than they
otherwise would have been. John was the
first to enjoy a joke, even when levelled in
fun against himself.

There was a small local paper, published

each week, in the newly-rising township,
and a cartoonist amused the settlers by
inserting caricatures of local celebrities. One
week, soon after his arrival, John White's
picture appeared. He stood there, a small
man, dressed in conventional missionary
attire. By his side was a large pail of white-
wash, and in his hand a brush. A massive
African figure stood opposite, and beneath
the cartoon was written, " Don't worry, I'll
make you *white*."

John's fund of practical common sense
brought him through the hardships of those
days without a further breakdown in health.
As he faced every difficulty and danger his
spirits began to rise rather than to fall. The
serious illness from which he had suffered
passed away.

While he thus dealt severely with his own
countrymen and also with his own weaknesses,
John was no less severe, though infinitely
patient, with the vices of the Mashona tribes-
men themselves. For he loved them far
too dearly to indulge in mere sentiment, or
draw fanciful pictures about them. He never
minimised or made light of anything which
he saw to be evil. Above all, the cruelties
connected with the witch doctors roused his
indignation. They seemed to carry with

them the spirit of devilry and to make human beings into fiends.

Nor did John fail to remember the utter wretchedness in which the Mashona tribes had existed before, owing to the fierce Matabele raids. Driven into the caves of the earth, year after year, and hunted like wild animals, the Mashona had become a fear-stricken, torture-racked people.

It was because his sense of justice among his own fellow-countrymen was so high and his faith in Christ was so strong, that John could not endure any injustice when he saw it committed by those who professed and called themselves Christians. At the same time, he felt a deep and sincere sympathy for the British settlers as they led their isolated lives in lonely places, where every temptation was at hand to entice them to evil. He understood the danger they were in and was tender-hearted, with a love that suffered long and was kind.

But public and official injustice he could not endure. He spoke out, with burning words of rebuke, whenever he came up against it.

CHAPTER V : THE MASHONA REBELLION

JOHN WHITE always believed that the revolt of such an unwarlike people as the Mashona need never have happened, if only the treatment of them by the early settlers had been more humane and just. During the two years before the rebellion, while he lived among the Mashona and was called Baba (Father) by everyone who met him, he found out how their minds were filled with perpetual suspicion and fear. As the healer of their sick and the teacher of their children, he could win their affection. Above all, the love of Christ, burning in his own heart, made him sympathise with them so deeply, that his own love for them was wonderfully returned. For they came at last to trust no one as they trusted Baba White. They would gladly have laid down their lives for him, if occasion had required.

But even he was taken by surprise when the rebellion suddenly broke out in 1896. The Matabele were accustomed to fighting, but the Mashona were known to shrink from it. Apart from the witch doctors, who had come over secretly from the Matabele, they would hardly have risen in revolt.

John was on his way from Fort Victoria when the fighting began. He had brought the Rev. Isaac Shimmin with him, who had been held up on account of a break-down in transport. The first news of the Mashona revolt reached him near Salisbury, which had been immediately turned into a laager, or military camp, and placed under a commandant.

It was realised at once that the rising was serious. Information was at first very scanty. News was brought in by letter that a party of Europeans had been cut off in the Mazoe Valley. John White and Stanlake at once set out on bicycles to reconnoitre. They went forward in scouting fashion all through the night ; but when the first light of dawn appeared it was evident that they had been discovered. To go forward was clearly impossible and John's coolness in the face of danger saved the situation. He suggested a dash back to Salisbury, before they were surrounded, and they accomplished this safely, bringing valuable news with them.

Before any help could arrive, many of the evangelists and teachers who had been trained by John White were massacred, along with isolated Europeans. James Anta, a Zulu evangelist, was killed with all his family; his church and school were burnt to the ground.

When the full history of Mashonaland is written by some historian in the future, it may be found that James Anta and his family, who thus suffered for their faith, were the first in the noble army of martyrs drawn from the young Church of the Mashona among whom Christ's name has so recently been made known. He had been a faithful witness to the power of the Gospel and his brave spirit never shrank when the call came. Others were soon to follow in his train ; and their blood, thus freely shed, was to be the seed of the harvest, which was reaped in later years.

The people at Chiremba's Kraal, and at Epworth Farm, who had come into closest touch with John White, were getting restive. John went out to them and they asked him to be spokesman on their behalf with the Government, so that they might be allowed to stay near the laager, outside the town of Salisbury, under protection. John promised them this, and kept his word.

But a rumour went round the camp that their loyalty was doubtful and the commandant was urged to send them back to

their own kraals. John went immediately
to head-quarters and explained that it was
through him they had sought protection and
that he would stand surety for their loyalty.
He added, " If you send these people back
to be at the mercy of the rebels, I must go
with them." The commandant wisely allowed
them to stay.

Then a fear grew up among the Mashona
themselves, who had come in for protection,
that they might be massacred by the Europeans. In order to reassure them, John said,
" I will sleep each night among you, outside
the laager, so that if they come to kill you,
they will kill me also."

This was one of the quiet deeds of love
whereby John gained at last the complete
confidence of the Mashona people. His word
from that time forth was regarded as the
word of truth.

It is interesting to note that a similar
incident occurred at Agra, in India, during
the early days of the Indian Mutiny. Dr.
Valpy French declared that he would go
outside and suffer with the Indian Christians,
if they were refused protection within the
Fort. He won his case, just as John White
did, by this notable act of moral courage.

During this period of terrible distress and

danger, John White saw one day a Christian woman in great pain approaching the laager along with her two daughters. To his alarmed surprise, he found that it was the wife of John Molele, the evangelist, whom he had left at the village of Nengubo. The two daughters had brought in their mother with great difficulty. They told John their sad but heroic story.

Molele had received a note from the evangelist, Ramushu, at Chiremba's Kraal, saying that the Mashona were rising in rebellion all over the country and that he should seek immediate shelter with his family and fellow Christians at the laager in Salisbury.

But just at the same time, Molele received another message from a European settler, named James White, who lived eight miles away, telling him that the rebels had come and killed his companion and that he himself had been wounded in the leg, so that he could not get away. Would Molele therefore come across and put him on a wagon and bring him over to the mission station at Nengubo ?

The situation was in every way desperate. If Molele attempted to save the settler, James White, he would almost certainly forfeit his own life and that of his family. Yet he did not hesitate. Molele went in a wagon to James White's farm, bound up his leg and set out on his journey back to the Mission at Nengubo.

When, however, the wagon had reached within a mile, shots rang out and they were ambushed. James White, the settler, urged Molele to save his own life and those of his family and leave him to die ; for it seemed impossible for him to escape with his wounded leg. But Molele refused. The Mashona rushed forward. Molele was killed first and then the spearmen rushed right in and speared James White to death. After this, they violently drove forward Molele's wife and children to be done to death in the mission church. Two of his daughters fled and hid themselves ; but the little sons of Molele, with their mother, could not escape. The boys were killed outright in cold blood, and the mother was speared and left for dead.

When the darkness of night came on, the two girls crept back to the village and found that their mother had regained consciousness. Travelling through the night on foot and hiding by day, they reached Salisbury and showed themselves to " Baba " White. It had taken them four days to reach Salisbury, a distance of fifty miles. Molele's wife had to make the journey in great pain with the spear wound still unhealed

Later on, when all the fighting was ended, John White went on foot to Nengubo and gathered together the remains of the settler James White and the brave Molele with his little children. He buried them under the shelter of a great tree near to the spot where he had found them and placed over them a wooden cross.

Very near to the grave of these martyred ones John's own ashes lie to-day among the Mashona people. The graves of African teachers and evangelists are grouped together side by side. Around this sacred spot, the institute, called Waddilove, has been built up by the prayers and labours of John and his wife along with the faithful band of those who have worked with him. During thirty years, with different breaks through illness, his African home was either here or at Epworth Farm, and it was to this home that he brought his wife, as a fellow worker, quite early in the history of the institution.

Towards the end of the rebellion, John White gave fearless expression to his conviction that the disaster was in a large measure due to the injustice which had crept

into the administration.   This was an opinion
that at once brought him into public controversy, and his name was made prominent
as one who condemned his fellow countrymen.
But he never shrank from what he knew to
be the truth.

The subject of the treatment of the African
is so important, not only for Southern
Rhodesia, but for every other Colony, or
Protectorate, where European rule prevails,
that I shall quote, with only slight abbreviation, John's carefully written statement about
the causes of the rebellion, which he sent
to the *Methodist Times*, in London.   This
article was widely commented on, both in
Great Britain and also in South Africa.
Perhaps no public utterance in his whole
career carried such weight with it as this.

Before quoting, however, from John's
article, I would like to add, in a parenthesis,
that throughout this book I have avoided as
far as possible the use of the word " native,"
as a noun, either in the singular or plural,
and have substituted for it the tribal word
" Mashona," or the wider name " African."

For among the educated classes, especially,
both in India and in Africa, there is a growing
dislike of this word, which is supposed,
rightly or wrongly, to carry something of

contempt with it when used by Europeans.
In earlier days, this was not felt or noticed,
but the feeling against the use of the word
has been growing stronger and stronger in
recent years.

In India, the use of the word "native"
has now been entirely forbidden in official
documents, and though the dislike has not
gone so far as this in Africa, yet it is undoubtedly increasing. The Christian Church
ought, therefore, to anticipate such an act
of courtesy as this, while seeking in every
word and deed to follow the Golden Rule of
Christ.

In John White's own time there was no
discourtesy either felt or intended. Nevertheless, since it is my great hope that this
book will be read widely in Africa among
African Christians for many years to come,
and also translated, I have ventured to drop
the word, even in quotations, and to use
tribal names instead.

John White writes in his article as follows :
"Now that the back of the Mashona
Rebellion is broken we are better able to
give a dispassionate opinion of the affair.
I, personally, have refrained hitherto from
committing myself publicly, because I wanted
to hear what would be assigned as the cause

of the rebellion. . . . The local Press has now spoken. It declares that the Mashona have been treated in the past with too much decency. . . . The contention, that cruelty to the Mashona has had anything to do with the rising, has been described as a ' cruel, cowardly and wicked lie.' We are thus compelled, even though reluctantly, to state the truth as we believe it.

" Last year an instance was reported to me where one of the officials used the influence of his position to obtain a girl for immoral purposes. By threats of punishment, he compelled the Chief to give him his own daughter. I brought the matter to the notice of the administration, and the accused was found guilty of the charge. Shortly after, he left the country ; yet so trivial seemed the offence that within nine months he was back again and held an official position in the force raised to punish the rebels.

" Another glaring act of official injustice and cruelty was committed in 1894. A policeman, named Cooper, was murdered by a great chief, Mamziva Zuba. Under the Sub-Inspector of Police a force was sent out to punish the murderer or murderers. At that time the Rev. G. Eva was in charge of the Presbyterian Mission Station some thirty miles south of the place. One Sunday, this force arrived at his station just as he was concluding the service. According to previous arrangement a number of surrounding chiefs had gathered there for the day. The officer in charge ordered the chiefs, seven in number, to be arrested. Without in any way fastening them, they were told that if they attempted to run away they would be shot. Then they moved on. About five minutes later, Mr. Eva heard a shot and ran to see what was the matter. He found that only three of the chiefs were with the force ; three had been shot, and one had escaped. The officer, by way of explaining, said, ' Your chiefs have run away. I am very sorry for what has happened.' Mr. Eva declares, ' I am prepared to swear on oath that these chiefs were absolutely innocent of the policeman's death. Indeed, they were at that time totally ignorant of its occurrence and did not know of it until I told them.' Thus on the pretext of their running away, three innocent chiefs lost their lives. Although this was reported to the Government nothing was done.

" Very often great injustice has been done to the Mashona people by the way in which the Hut Tax has been collected. In the

collecting of this rarely any attempt is made
to levy the charge equitably. This has had
the tendency to make the Mashona discon-
tented and the Hut Tax hated. In many
districts, where previously considerable herds
of cattle were to be found, now hardly one
exists. I do not say that the Hut Tax
ought to be discontinued; I do think,
however, some just and less repulsive method
of collecting ought to be devised.

"The above cases are typical. Such in-
justices have had a tendency to make the
Mashona fear and hate the Government and
most of its officials.

"A little time ago, the Government enlisted
and trained a large number of Mashona and
Matabele police. They were placed under
the control of the Commissioners. Previously
these fellows were arrant cowards. Once
they are mounted with a little authority
and a rifle, they develop into tyrants. One
night I was travelling north and arrived late
at a kraal and was preparing to sleep outside,
when the chief, who happened to know me,
offered me a hut for myself and carriers.
About midnight I awoke, with some half-
dozen people rushing into my place, who
told me that a policeman had attempted to
force his way into the hut where the women

were sleeping. I have since gathered that assaults on women by these scoundrels are of frequent occurrence. So evil has become the reputation of these representatives of official justice, that their arrival at a kraal is the occasion of the worst alarms. Recently, when the Matabele chiefs were arranging terms of surrender, they mentioned, as one of the causes of the revolt, their treatment by certain Government officials, but especially the African police.

" Scattered throughout the country are a considerable number of settlers. The attitude of many of these had been humane and just. Others, however, have given the Mashona a very poor opinion of civilised justice and propriety. Many of them have bought, according to African custom, Kaffir girls whom they regard as their property. The girls consider themselves, to all intents and purposes, the slaves of these men. In consequence, before many years elapse the Government will be confronted with a very serious social problem, unless it puts an end to this sort of thing at once.

" Put these foregoing facts together and then let me ask you whether the charge of injustice to the Africans is a ' cruel, cowardly and wicked lie.'

" ' We had better be dead,' some of them said, ' than be tormented like this ! '

" For two or three seasons unusually large swarms of locusts have visited the country, and this year a terrible cattle plague has swept through the land. As is their custom, these Mashona, when they need advice, resort to the medium of their gods. The witch doctors then make an inquiry from the Murenga—great spirit. ' If you want to get rid of your trouble,' the witch doctors reply, ' you must kill the white men.'

" Such advice was atrociously cruel and fearfully indiscriminate. But think for a moment ! These people are utterly savage and reason accordingly. The witch doctors are actually shrewd and cunning. Dr. Jameson had taken away a number of mounted troops. Then, when off our guard, the naturally cowardly Mashona rose in one dark mass, carrying death and desolation.

" Will the Chartered Company see its mistake and make an honest attempt to mend matters ? We must not forget the many good qualities of the Company. As a church they have treated us handsomely. Their occupation of the territory has done much to advance civilisation in Central Africa ' They have brought many things within easier

reach of the Africans. Those things we
cannot overlook.

" At present the land is under a dark
cloud ; confusion and strife reign everywhere   Let those in authority see the position with honest hearts. Where corruption
or injustice is found, let them sweep it away,
laying the foundation of righteousness and
truth. Then we feel sure a bright and
successful future awaits us."

After such a public statement written to
the Press in Great Britain, John's position
among the Europeans became more difficult
than ever. " If," he writes to his friend,
" there is to-day a more unpopular man in
Mashonaland than John White, I would like
to meet him ! The local papers have gone
out of their way to revile me. I was informed the other day that there were a
hundred men in this colony who were ready
to blow my brains out if they could get the
chance ! "

A short story about John White during
the rebellion has been given by Mr. Fitt,
of Gatooma. " While stationed," he writes,
" at Fort Charter, friendly Mashona, belonging to the mission stations controlled by
Mr. White, reported that they were being
attacked by the rebels. A mounted patrol

was at once dispatched, John White accom-
panying it and acting as guide. The Mashona,
though friendly, were evidently alarmed at
the approach of armed men and thought
that they were being mistaken for rebels and
were being punished.

" After a shot had been fired at the patrol,
the latter halted, and John White volunteered
to go alone on foot to assure them. The
result was that their Mashona evangelist also
detached himself from the frightened body
of men with him and met John. When it
was seen that they were shaking hands, the
Mashona were satisfied and the patrol spent
the night at the Mission."

Not once alone, but many times over, John
became peacemaker in this fashion during
the last stages of the rebellion. Often, by
running serious risks, he succeeded in saving
human life.

Belesi, one of John White's evangelists,
was in charge of Kwenda School. When the
rebellion broke out the rebels conspired to
kill him and the chief gave his consent. But
at this point one of the men, who had visited
the school, advised the chief to think of the
consequences that would follow if he put him
to death. He told the chief how, every day,
Belesi gathered the children and called them

all by their names, and how he never forgot to call even those who were absent. This showed that Belesi knew all their children by name. If he were killed, his spirit might return and call to death all their children, one by one, as he used to do in school.

This story had a devastating effect upon the chief. He was so excited that he ordered Belesi to be brought, and at once deprived him of his European dress. He then ordered him to dress in the fashion of the kraal and bade him sit down in the courtyard under his protection. Thus his life was saved.

Towards the end of this terrible conflict, in which so many of his own children in the faith had suffered and he himself had been so near to death, John sent a touching letter to a friend in one of his own Cumberland dales :

" I fancy," he wrote, " that the worst is over now and we shall come out of this trouble. It would be a great treat to get away from all this strife for a time to some quiet spot where we could be clear of all these things. What a pleasure it would be to be among all my old friends at Workington ! But this pleasure must be denied me for a time. If Providence puts me in the front of the strife, it would be arrant cowardice to abandon the post of duty."

The last sentence fills me with deep emotion when I read it, knowing John White as I did. For in the last years of his life his eyes used to gaze out of the window of his sick-room and fill with tears as he thought of spring-time in his own loved Cumberland dales, knowing that he would never see them again. He was a brave fighter, even to the last, but his heart had the tenderness of a little child, and a touch of home, with its childhood's memories, always brought this tenderness to the front.

CHAPTER VI : THE TWO KINGDOMS

WE have a vivid picture of John White drawn by the Rev. M. Gautrey, which brings him before us as he appeared to others during his pioneer work in Mashonaland.

"He stood in the clear sunlight of an African morning, a short, sturdy, workman-like figure. A pair of jack-boots covered his feet and reached half-way up his shins ; a pair of riding breeches covered the lower part of him. Thorn bushes had made havoc at the knees ; a shirt, open at the throat, revealed the fair white skin below the rim of tan. His beard had known no razor for a month and was trying to curl all ways at once. A broad-brimmed hat failed entirely to conceal the shock of tousled hair."

After the first overthrow of the rebellion, John decided at once to visit all the mission stations. This journey, undertaken alone, was full of danger ; for pillage and massacre, along with fierce guerrilla warfare, were still continuing, which meant that he took his life in his hands, as he went from one kraal to another.

At one village, where the chief had received John hospitably for the night, the rebels swept down later, killed eighteen men, burned down their huts, and carried off their women, children and cattle.

At another kraal, on the border of the rebels' country, John was received with loud protestations of friendship.

" What do you think now," asked John, " of Murenga, the great spirit ? What has he done for you, his followers ? "

" Murenga," replied the chief, " has deceived us. He has lied."

" Then if Murenga lies," John answered, " is it not time that you turned to the true God ? "

But many inveterate evils would have to be put away if the true God was to be worshipped. Was the chief prepared to count the cost ?

At one village John contracted a bad attack of malarial fever, and had the greatest difficulty, when the fever grew less, in reaching the hospital at Salisbury ; for he had neither horse nor wagon, and was obliged to go all the way on foot.

Yet amid much that was disheartening and had led to a breakdown in the work, there were other things that were most

encouraging. He found teachers who were
prepared to go out at the peril of their lives
even where the revolt was not over. Just
as he, John, was ready to risk his life for
Christ's sake, so were they ready to risk
theirs. In such a dark time of spiritual
depression nothing gave him more encouragement than this.

" They are there now," John writes, " quite
unprotected, save by God. The other day
a messenger came from one of the ex-rebel
villages asking us to send an evangelist, for
they were anxious to learn the new religion.
One of the teachers was free, and he went
at once. In a few weeks I am going down
to see how he fares."

There is one word of St. Paul, written to
the Church at Philippi, which seems exactly
to describe John's attitude during these days
when the rebellion was still smouldering and
the whole future of the mission work in
Mashonaland seemed to be hanging in the
balance.

" Forgetting those things that are behind,"
St. Paul writes, " and reaching forth unto
those things that are before, I press towards
the mark for the prize of the high calling
of God in Christ Jesus." [1]

[1] Phil. iii. 13.

Where others might have been discouraged at seeing so much good work overthrown, John was all for pressing forward. He saw beyond the Mashona country a vaster hinterland ahead, where the great Zambesi River continually beckoned him onward.

Biographers have often pointed to the eager gaze of Cecil Rhodes, as he also looked north towards the Zambesi. There, through the open corridor of Bechuanaland, according to Rhodes, lay the highway to empire and commerce which must never be allowed to be closed.

In the gardens at Cape Town, near the House of Assembly, where Rhodes often used to speak on this very theme, his statue is erected. He stands, a tall, rough-hewn figure, with his arm outstretched towards the north. The words, " Your Hinterland lies there," are graven on the plinth beneath the statue.

Rhodes's dreams were of a concrete, earthly kingdom, and he adopted the means which he believed would most quickly accomplish his end.

How different was the Dominion of Christ, for which John White was straining every nerve and utilising every moment !

It was hardly a mere coincidence that the two efforts in the Divine Providence were

destined to take place simultaneously and to
lead to such different results. The "kingdoms
of this world," in their material shape and
form, were being fought for and lost and won
amid a welter of slaughter. The "kingdoms
of our Lord and of His Christ" were being
established by incredible sacrifice and suffering, with no reliance upon human power at
all, but with full trust in the power of the
Living God.

Cecil Rhodes and John White! They
crossed each other's paths from time to time
but rarely met in person. The contrast
between the two men hardly needs em-
phasising. It is patent to all. Rhodes chose
deliberately his own peculiar weapons in
order to gain his material success. John
White discarded these weapons and trusted
in God alone.

Yet though the contrast was clear-cut and
sharply distinct, there was also an element
where the two characters drew towards each
other. For below the surface, in Cecil Rhodes's
nature, there was a deep vein of idealism,
inherited perhaps from the country rectory
in Suffolk, where he was born, and heightened
by his devotion to Oxford, where he came
back again and again to study.

There was also a greatness in the way that

Cecil Rhodes brought to an end by peaceful means at last the misery of the rebellion. The story, how he went unarmed day after day to meet the rebels in the Matoppo Hills, near Bulawayo, is a noble one which cannot be repeated too often.

He had sent messengers ahead to the Paramount Chief, who was still keeping the rebellion alive and continuing guerilla warfare. After a week's delay the messengers came back with the message that if Rhodes himself would come unarmed, with no more than three companions, also unarmed, a parley might be held.

Rhodes immediately consented and went forward. " Is it peace ? " he asked.

" It is peace," was the reply.

But the grievances, which had to be righted, seemed to be never ending, and the parley went on day by day. With wonderful patience Rhodes continued his peace mission, entirely trusting himself and his companions into the enemies' hands.

Then at last, when a final parley had been called, Rhodes found himself, as he rode up, surrounded by armed men with assegais pointed towards him. He dismounted and thus placed himself entirely at their mercy.

" What is this ? " he asked.

The countermanding order was given and the weapons were laid aside. Now the final parley was held. Day after day it went on, almost interminably, but Rhodes's patience was never exhausted. At last peace was declared.

Rhodes kept his promises as far as he possibly could. He gave the late enemies food for their starving people. He partly disbanded the African police, who had driven the tribes into rebellion by their cruelties and exactions. He did away with certain evils in the administration. He also compensated the European settlers wherever he could do so for the losses they had sustained. In order to carry out these things he placed large sums of his own private income at the disposal of the Chartered Company.

But even Cecil Rhodes himself could not keep under control the troopers who were patrolling the country on horseback and beating out the dying embers of revolt. Excesses were committed, under what was virtually martial law, wherein the innocent were confused with the guilty.

John White met, as he went about the country, instances of gross injustice and openly bore witness against them as a true and faithful follower of Jesus Christ, his

Lord and Master. Just as he had spoken plainly about the causes of the revolt, so now he condemned these excesses. The inevitable consequence of this was that he became more disliked than ever by many of the European settlers, while others greatly admired his courage.

The meanest of all accusations was now levelled against him by an anonymous writer. An unsigned letter, which received wide publicity, charged him with having saved his own skin by retiring to the laager at Salisbury. It also accused the African Christians of treacherously joining in the revolt.

Anyone who knew John at all was aware of the gross libel of such a charge as this, for no one who had ever met him could think of him as a coward. But there were some who did not know him personally; and among such, accusations of this kind could do incredible harm. John decided to answer. The accusation of treachery also, which was brought against the African Christians, stung him to the quick.

All through what I have attempted to write the refrain will run, which can hardly be too often repeated, that the real power John had among the Mashona people, so that they trusted him beyond anyone they had ever known before, was due to his deep love of them in Christ, his Lord. It was an echo of that " amazing love " which Christ had for him, John White, when He died for him upon the Cross :

> Love so amazing, so divine,
> Demands my soul, my life, my all.

John not only joined in singing those words in church ; he lived them in his daily life, and realised them amid all the sufferings he had to bear. He truly could say with the apostle :

" In weariness and painfulness, in watchings often, in hunger and thirst, in fastings often, in cold and nakedness,

" Beside those things that are without, that which cometh upon me daily, the care of all the churches.

" Who is weak, and I am not weak ? Who is offended and I burn not ? "[1]

For he burnt with indignation, kindled at the pure flame of love, when his own Mashona disciples were thus defamed and vilified by this unknown writer in the Rhodesian newspaper.

" Ordinarily," he replied to his anonymous

[1] 2 Cor. ii. 28, 29.

accuser, " I should treat such accusations with the silent contempt they deserve. But this time, I will put my scruples aside and answer them."

John then goes on to reply in detail to the different charges, and especially to answer the cruel accusation brought against the Mashona Christians. In the end he asks the writer to come out into the open and fight fairly. Let him reveal his name.

To take any notice at all of such baseless accusations as these was altogether distasteful to John White. For his nature was chivalrous and generous to an extraordinary degree. Conflicts like these, against subtle falsehoods, wore him out far more than all his physical labours. They came also at a time when the spiritual strain, that had been constantly oppressing him during the rebellion, had made him peculiarly sensitive. For after his earlier illness he was still in danger of a nervous breakdown, as he knew to his cost.

Thus while the spiritual struggle was against the powers of darkness on every side, John met it, as I have explained, not by giving way to it, either in himself or in others, but rather by pointing forward.

The Zambesi River was ahead, and it must

be reached and crossed ! The Gospel must be proclaimed in Central Africa ! This was the will of God and it should be accomplished !

"The widespread spiritual destitution," he writes, "shortly after the rebellion, is an eloquent, if dumb, appeal to the whole Church *to go forward* ! If the work of God is to revive and grow, two things are urgently needed :

"(1) A complete devotion to Christ on the part of all our workers.

"(2) A speedy multiplication of workers to supplement the duties of the regular Ministry.

"There is only one way whereby these two necessary results can be brought about— Prayer ! "

Again he writes home to his friend, " Please God, we shall cross the Zambesi before I see you again ! "

Thus with a high courage, when everything around looked black with storm and defeat, he kept the banners flying. *Vexilla Regis prodeunt* he might truly have said—" The Royal Banners forward go."

This sense of pressing forward made him eager to find out whether anything in himself was impeding the final victory. It was typical of John's humility to do this, and he discovered within his heart a lack of full charity towards those Europeans, who had grown so hostile to him. In his eagerness to champion the African cause, he felt that he had neglected them and had not considered enough their great need.

"I notice," he writes, "that the sainted David Hill, of China, spent many of his spare moments in visiting European officials and others, seeking to gain their friendship and to make them interested in his work.

"It is undoubtedly the best method. It was Christ's method, as distinguished from that of John the Baptist."

, It was not, however, till a later period in his life, when he was stationed for a time at Bulawayo, that he was able to carry out his full intentions and devote more time to the needs of the European settlers. This will come later in the story. At the time in his life that we have now reached, he had strained to the utmost point of endurance his physical powers, while he endured hardness as a good soldier of Jesus Christ, his Master.[1]

[1] 2 Timothy ii. 3.

FOR a long time after the Mashona rebellion had become a thing of the past, John still went on leading a life of incessant travel, visiting the different mission stations.

He had often to follow his Master quite literally, as he wandered without a home, moving from one village to another, having nowhere to lay his head—cheering, encouraging, helping and fostering the young Christian community which looked upon him as their Father.

The words which our Lord Himself quoted at Nazareth, concerning His own ministry, might also describe at this time the ministry of John as he tried to follow in his Master's steps :

" The Spirit of the Lord is upon me, because He hath anointed me to preach the Gospel to the poor : He hath sent me to heal the broken-hearted, to preach deliverance to the captives, and recovering of sight to the blind, to set at liberty them that are bruised, to proclaim the acceptable year of the Lord."

For John's great work was to heal and

restore ; to bind up the wounds that the rebellion had caused.

Though the life was excessively hard and often desperately disappointing, yet John's humour had play in his letters :

" I have slept," he writes, " in some funny places before, but I think that this occasion was the worst !

" One night we came late to a village whose people were unknown to me. We had been on foot since six in the morning and now it was eight o'clock in the evening. You can guess how tired we were ! I asked the chief if he could let us have a hut to sleep in, and he gave us a small place not more than ten feet across. Five goats were in residence when I retired, and these, an evangelist, four carriers and myself slept together in this awful place !

" I was glad when dawn came. But should I grumble, when the Son of Man had not where to lay His head ?

" For a long time I have been living a kind of gipsy life, moving about perpetually from place to place. To say that I like it is scarcely true. My joy is found in treading the path of duty. Unless something unforeseen happens, I shall be doing this kind of work for the next two years.

" I have just returned from a fortnight's tour to some of the stations north-west of here. The point reached farthest north was about three days' trek from the Zambesi River ! It is my plan, if God spares me, to cross that mighty river before I return home ! "

This thought of reaching the Zambesi is often repeated in the correspondence to his friend, the Rev. H. Needham, to whom I am indebted for the use of these letters.

" For sixty miles," he continues, " I travelled by bullock-wagon, leaving it finally at a mission farm. Then I got carriers and went to some kraals farther on. How I wish you could have done that walk with me ! We tramped on an average about twenty miles a day. The last week I did over 120 miles, in a climate where the temperature was over 100 degrees in the shade. It was very hard going.

" One day, in particular, I shall never forget. We had travelled from sunrise to noon, having had very little food. The sand was so hot that you could not bear your hand upon it. The gun-barrel on my shoulder was equally hot. I could only hold it by the stock. The wind might have come from a furnace. How I reached the next village I

really do not know. It was the cruellest
walk I have ever had.

" The people I found to be absolute heathen.
The chief hindrance to the work is the kind
of white men they meet sometimes—either
mounted police, hunters or traders. Some
take their women, others take their produce
without giving adequate payment : and when
some have protested, they have been shot
down like buck. I can verify this. . . .

" While I am writing, there is a big dance
going on about three hundred yards away.
It is called the Mashabi. Whatever they
need on this occasion they wish for, and it is
supposed to come. Many of them must be
rather mild in their wishes, for they don't
get much ! The dance is, of course, accompanied by a big ' beer drink.'

" There is something very sad about the
whole business. But their hearts are as
hungry as ours for the Bread of Life. Yet
many are satisfied with the husks. May the
Father of our Lord Jesus Christ give them
the true Bread sent down from heaven."

The work which he had to accomplish
from place to place during these journeyings
was often sad and discouraging, with here
and there a bright gleam of sunshine.

" At the place I visited recently," he writes,

" I found the evangelist very low-spirited.
A year ago he had eighty children in the
school, and now he has only half that number.
' The locusts,' he said, ' have eaten up all
our crops. We shall soon die of starvation.
So what is the use of attending to religious
things ? ' "

On the other hand, John found encouragement at other mission stations. " A fortnight ago," he writes, " I left a place eighty
miles from here. I found the people all eager
to learn . . . We held a prayer meeting at
4.45 a.m. and nearly a hundred were present.
In the evening four people expressed deep
sorrow for their sins and decided to take
Christ as their Saviour.

" All this has taken place at a spot where
only two years ago the people were absolute
heathen. It is God's work, and to Him be
the glory."

One of the stories of his devotion to the
Mashona people, which is often told among
them, runs as follows : While he was paying
a visit to Kwenda Mission in an ox-wagon,
he found the evangelist Tutani and his wife
and family lying ill. Since their condition
appeared serious and there was no doctor
nearer than Salisbury, which was 150 miles
distant, he made the ox-wagon as comfortable

as possible and placed the whole family inside, telling the drivers to proceed to Salisbury by easy stages.

He himself went on foot as quickly as he could. There were flooded rivers to cross and the journey on foot was most trying. He came to Salisbury some days ahead of the ox-wagon and sent back runners with medicine and food. Thus the remainder of the journey was made by the sick family with greater comfort and they all recovered. John was well known after that as the Father who would make any sacrifice for his children.

A quaint account of Baba White's way of winning the confidence of the Mashona is told us by Andrew Shamu, a Christian.

" Baba White," he says, " found us residing on a very cold spot, where there were no trees growing. He brought us on to the place of warmth. When he reached our village, people called him Giwa (walker) as he did all his journeys on foot.

" He went about the villages on foot, teaching and preaching. Wherever he went, people at first held him in deep suspicion. They said : ' What does this Giwa want in our villages ? '

" When he came to Nengubo he built a small school and ordered a teacher to help

him. As he made us Christians, he always
said to us: ' Pray, looking to the north over
the Zambesi, where there are people like you
who have never heard the message about
God.'

" As time went on the number of schools
and teachers increased. We wondered how
he managed to travel from place to place
on foot, as there were no roads in those days.

" In the first place, we always saw him
walking, then we saw him riding a pony ;
thirdly we saw him on a bicycle. Afterwards
he rode in a cart, and last of all in a motor.
Of course, he could visit many places in a
shorter time by motor, when the roads were
made.

" One day we had camped and a white
traveller reached our tent. As it was getting
very dark Baba asked him to share our tent,
but the white man refused. So he went on
towards Salisbury.

" Later on this traveller felt very tired and
took off his boots and put them at his feet
as he lay down to sleep under a tree. Before
very long a lion came and made off with his
boots. So he had to run back to our tent
and reached it, trembling from head to foot.
' If you had only listened,' said Baba, ' you
would not have had all this trouble.'

" So Baba White offered him his own spare
shoes, but they would not fit, because Baba
was much smaller than this big man. So he
had to go limping along till we reached
Salisbury together."

" In another part of the country," John
writes, " I had an adventure at one of the
large swollen rivers. I was travelling with
the wagonette of a friend of mine. We had
our things in the wagonette and were ourselves travelling on horseback.

" One night, just at sundown, we came to
a river. When we had passed eastward
about ten days before, the river was quite
fordable and we had managed to get over
without any difficulty. But now it was a
raging torrent.

" My companion was an experienced
traveller and when I expressed my doubt
about the safety of attempting the crossing,
he assured me that there was no need to be
afraid. Our food and bedding were all in
the wagonette and we were behind.

" The mules went into the river, but the
leader, starting to swim, was unable to get
the others to follow after, and so they became
mixed up in the river. The torrent carried
everything down stream. The mules were all
drowned ; the drivers escaped. But all our

stuff was wasted and our wagon was right away down-stream.

" All through that night it poured with rain. My friend and I took what rest we could under a tree. The result was that my companion got a bad attack of fever, from which fortunately I escaped. Such things as these were constantly happening during those early days when I travelled to and fro."

One last story of John's life as a wanderer at this time may complete the picture !

He had determined to meet his colleagues in Salisbury at Christmas in 1895. It was the middle of the rainy season. Frequently the wagon wheels would sink deep in the mud and at last, on Christmas Eve, they came to a boggy patch where all four wheels were stuck fast. The oxen could not shift it any farther and the rain was pouring down in torrents. They outspanned the oxen and took them into the shelter of a cave in a kopje not far away. Soaked to the skin, John went back to the wagon, and when Christmas morning dawned, after a sleepless night, he saw all around him an inland lake in the midst of which the wagon was marooned. The driver had taken shelter in the cave, and there was nothing for it but to remain all through Christmas Day under those conditions.

These adventures, with fever following hard upon them were not unusual in those early days in Southern Rhodesia, when good metalled roads were not in existence and an ox-wagon was the only method of conveyance.

CHAPTER VIII : CHIREMBA'S KRAAL

MORE and more clearly as John White went on labouring and toiling, certain vital and essential needs began to stand out in his mind above all others, until they were indelibly stamped upon it.

The first was the need of the written Word, understood and read continually by the Mashona tribes in their own mother tongue.

The second was the need of evangelists and teachers, trained and disciplined in reliance upon the Holy Spirit of God—men and women who should go forth among their own people to bear witness by the purity of their lives and the devotion of their hearts to Christ as their Lord and Saviour.

The third was to keep the young Church rooted and grounded in' the very soil of the country. It must not be a foreign and exotic thing, out of touch with genuine African life as it had been lived in the village kraals for countless generations. While the kraals must be made Christian in every single social aspect, their structure must not be abandoned for some other form of social life which the Mashona people could not understand.

It was a deeply-moving experience to me at Nengubo, where Waddilove Institution had been erected by John White, to find all these three aims still being actively attempted and John's work being carried on by his successors. On my short visit, I was given a copy of St. John's Gospel, translated by Baba White himself with the help of his students. The young evangelists were living in simple village fashion during their training, building with their own manual labour their own homes. The meeting hall and hospital were near at hand ; and in the centre of all was the House of God.

There, too, was the churchyard, where John's ashes had been reverently laid, close to the grave of Molele and his wife and children and James White, the settler, under the old tree. Others, too, were buried there, some from far-off England, some from Africa, side by side.

What patience of true devotion had gone to the making of that translation of St. John's Gospel ! What love had been put into this work of building a school for the young evangelists, who should help to bring Central Africa to the feet of Christ ! What new life in Christ had come to birth within the walls of this House of God, which pious hands had fashioned year after year ! Only those who are pioneers know how difficult, and yet how glorious, such creative work is.

The remembrance came back to me, while I was at Nengubo, of the story of the Venerable Bede and his young disciples—how he worked in his old age at the translation of St. John's Gospel during a time when paganism, with all its cruelties, prevailed in the British Isles. " It is finished," said the young scribe as the last verse was completed. " Thou sayest truly," said Bede. " It is finished." And his life's work was done.

The outward scenes were different—Saxon England and African Mashonaland—but the devotion for the Master was the same, and also the end in view. Out of that translation of the Gospel of Love in the Mashona's own language, a new and risen life, radiant with joy and hope, would spring forth in Central Africa as it did more than a thousand years ago in our own Northern Islands.

We have a picture of the pagan life at Nengubo before the Gospel came, given to us by one of the early Christian converts, who lived there during the evil days when human life was degraded to the lowest level.

" When Baba White," the writer states,
" first visited Nengubo he found the people
living like the beasts of the field. Many
evil things were being done in that village,
and many people refused to listen. But day
by day he visited our houses and ate with
us, and at night he slept in our village. The
first thing he taught us to do was to pray.
I remember well his first story. He told us
about the coming of the first man, Adam,
and his wife, Eve. He told us of the first
temptation and how many people sinned.
But he told us also about the forgiveness of
God and how that Jesus, His Son, called upon
all people to repent. These were great words
to our ears.

" My mother, Ruti Rwere, was the first
convert, and she put away her heathen
practices. Later, when the evangelist, John
Molele, came, many repented."

The story of John Molele's death has
already been told, and it was entirely fitting
that Nengubo should form the centre of the
work for training those who should follow
in his steps and become evangelists to their
own people.

Nothing but faith in the guidance and
power of God could have carried John through
the difficult times when Nengubo Institution

(now called Waddilove) was first planned and then erected. He had gone back from Africa to England for a much-needed furlough in 1898, but instead of resting at ease he used every spare moment of his time in putting before friends, who had sympathy with his plans, the outline of what he was contemplating. The sum of £150 was entrusted to him, and with this he determined to start. The pioneers in Africa, who worked with him, made their own bricks and built their own quarters. It was all a labour of love.

" Truly," wrote John, " it is a day of small things ! Our present tutorial staff is embodied entirely in myself ! But we have been led into this work by the hand of God, and we feel that it will grow into a great enterprise. . . . A few years ago, the youths whom we are now training were heathen. Is not this wonderful ? What a glorious object lesson of our Faith. Six years ago they were groping as blindly in darkness as their fathers were. But such is their change that they are now eager to become messengers of the glad tidings to others. To God be the glory ! Only His hand can work such wonders.

" Two of these youths belong to a large tribe living in the Zambesi Valley. The

younger, James Kamera, was converted in
our Christian Church at Salisbury. I asked
him one day what he would do if he were
trained. ' Well,' he said, ' my people have
no one to teach them. They are still living
in the dark. I should like to carry the
Gospel to them.'

" Another is the son of Chiremba, the chief
who lives at Epworth. Once a witch doctor,
now he and all his children are preparing to
be members with us and to receive Christian
training.

" One other comes from Barotseland, where
M. and Mme. Coillard have done such brave
pioneer work. He came to this country
seeking work and found the Saviour. Our
one object is to get hold of men whose hearts
God has touched."

Jonas Chiremba Chihota, the eldest of the
chief's sons, fired with a zeal for Christ,
went into a neighbouring pagan village to
preach the word of God. He denounced
their polygamy, their drunken feasts, their
witch doctors ; whereupon they beat him
half dead and sent him home. But he knew
no fear. On the next Sunday he went to
the same place and was beaten again. He
offered no resistance but remained in prayer
while the blows fell. The third time when

he went, they did not beat him at all. His faith and courage had been so great that they allowed him to preach without any hindrance.

Every spare hour that could be saved during John's journeys from village to village, and also while he was training the young evangelists at Nengubo, was given up to translating the Gospel.

" There was no literature at all," writes Moffat Gautrey, " in the language of the people he came to teach. The language itself had not been reduced to writing. Without the Gospel in their own tongue, how could they learn of the greatness of God's love and their heritage of salvation ?

" A packing-case formed his table, a soap box his seat, and a fruit tin his writing-pad planted between his Greek New Testament and a Revised English version. Then, with his wagon driver to help him with his vocabulary, he began the laborious task of translating those wonderful words of life and putting into the Mashona language the Stories of Jesus."

Jonas Chiremba Chihota was the wagon driver's name, who is mentioned above. As early as 1894, they began translating from St. Mark's Gospel together. When the oxen got tired they would outspan, and John White would take the Zulu Bible and by the help of Jonas translate it into the language of the Mashona. Most of his translation was done while he was on trek. What John had written down he revised and tested again and again. In the end, the help of the British and Foreign Bible Society was given and the different Gospels were published separately in London. They were then sent out to the Mashona, who flocked in to a centre to purchase them when it was known in the district that they had arrived.

The story of Chiremba himself must now be told. It is one of the most romantic in all John White's missionary career and led to the founding of Epworth Farm, near Salisbury, which formed his third great experiment.

When John first became friendly with Chiremba, the chief, the latter had five wives, and even practised as a witch doctor for private gain. Though he looked askance at the preachers who came to his kraal, Chiremba took a liking to John from the first and came to the church near the kraal whenever John himself took any service. On one occasion, that of a Christian marriage, Chiremba led the procession from the village

with the skin of an animal round his loins,
a light-coloured felt hat on his head, and
a jacket on which the letters " G.W.R." were
still visible, showing that it had been worn
on the Great Western Railway !

One day, Chiremba bought from a trader
a small looking-glass which could reflect the
rays of the sun on to the face of anyone
standing by. When this simple experiment
was shown, the people on whom the light of
the sun was reflected began to run in all
directions. But Chiremba saw a profitable
use that might be made of it. Calling together
the people belonging to a neighbouring village,
along with their chief, he said he would " smell
out " the thief who had stolen an ox. He
then deflected the light of the sun on the face
of a man who possessed a large number of
cattle. A panic ensued and the people fled
in all directions ; but soon a number of them
returned, leading with them an ox and
asking Chiremba to take it and remove the
magic from them.

Under the influence of John White, this
chief was brought to Christ by a growing
consciousness of sin. At first, his wives came
under the spell of the Gospel and asked to
be baptised. But this would mean that
Chiremba must give up his polygamous ways.

" The only thing for you to do," said Ramushu, the Christian minister, to Chiremba's wives, " is to pray for the conversion of your husband." They gave themselves to pray for his repentance.

Soon the memory of his past misdeeds came surging in upon him ; and so great was his spiritual distress that he cried aloud to God for deliverance. Every morning he would go out among the huge granite rocks and cast himself down on the ground in prayer, seeking salvation. All day long he would remain in agony of soul, till at last God heard his cry and set his soul at liberty.

With leaping and rejoicing, he came to see John. " Umfundisi," he cried, " I have been praying among the rocks and God has heard my prayer and made my heart clean."

" What shall I do ? " he asked.

" Go and talk it over with your wives," said John.

A suitable arrangement was made, by which Chiremba retained his first wife, according to the Christian law, and made provision for the rest.

The sacrifice that this would mean in prestige and power can hardly be imagined by those who have had no experience of life in an African kraal. But he made every sacrifice gladly for Christ's sake, and became a living witness to God's grace. He himself has passed away, but his family have proved themselves to be true servants of Christ. His eldest son, as we have seen, rendered valuable aid to John White in his translation of the New Testament ; and his grandson, Simon Chihota, is one of the most valued of the younger ministers in the Christian Church.

Chiremba's kraal is now well known, not only on account of the remarkable story of the conversion of Chiremba himself, but also because it forms the centre of Epworth Farm. This settlement of Christian families, united on a co-operative basis in a common social and religious life, formed the third, and in some ways the most interesting, of all John White's experiments. It grew out of his organising and directing powers, as he placed them under the guidance of the Holy Spirit, seeking to build up the kingdom of God's love in Africa. It is impossible in this brief volume to describe its history in detail. But some of the happiest years of John's life were spent there and some of his most fruitful work accomplished.

For there is probably nothing moıe important to remember in Africa to-day than the fact that the African is able to give out his best, both as an individual and in his family life, when his own close touch with the soil has not been broken. To sever that connexion with mother earth, is at once to create new and difficult problems. For this reason, an experiment such as Epworth Farm, and an institution such as that at Nengubo, represent efforts of the most fruitful kind, to build up the Christian Church in Mashonaland with its foundations truly laid.

CHAPTER IX : HIS MARRIED LIFE

No one could have been more devoted in her love and service to her husband, during the long months of suffering which accompanied John's last illness, than Mrs. White. It was my privilege to witness that devotion, and I shall write more about it in a subsequent chapter. Here, at this point in the narrative, the story of John's marriage needs to be briefly told, because from this time forward he had by his side a companion in the work that was set before him.

More and more it was brought home to him—so he told me the story—that it was not good for a man to be alone in such a work as he was now called upon to undertake, both as Chairman of the Mission District and also as the Governor of institutions such as Epworth Farm and Waddilove. He had been made Chairman in 1901. Thus there had come upon him the " care of all the churches."

Everywhere throughout the District he was sending forth into the villages his young evangelists, all of them married men. He longed to be able, as a married man himself, to give them fatherly advice and counsel. There was also needed at his side a wife to whom the young girls could go as a mother and receive motherly assistance. The missionary work which, in its earlier pioneer stage, almost demanded from him a homeless, wandering life, as he passed on trek from village to village, was now equally requiring from him a *home* life, if Epworth Farm and Waddilove were to be built up with Christian family life at their very centre.

" The responsibilities of the Chairmanship," he wrote, " trouble me little. It means more work, but if my health keeps good, the work is nothing, and worry I don't intend to know. I did not seek it. While I occupy the Chair, I will do my best, but won't fret if folks say that I have failed.

" *'Not failure, but low aim, is crime.'* "

Then follows, in another letter, the sad story such as every devoted servant of the Master may have to meet with love in his heart at some time or another, if he is a true shepherd of his flock seeking that which has gone astray until he find it.

" Returning from Umtali," he writes, " bad news awaited me. Petros, whom I trusted, has committed a grave sin. I was greatly

surprised and shocked ; indeed, I hardly
know yet where I am. The poor girl is not
to blame. When she came to me at night
to tell me she wept as though her heart would
break and I wept with her. Ah, Brigg, could
we but see the adverse side of the picture the
devil paints, we'd pause, wouldn't we ? . . .
Through this our reputation has been sacrificed and our work permanently injured."

Such incidents as these, which were not
unlikely to occur from time to time among
those who had come from surroundings where
things of this kind were common, made John
wish more than ever to have one by his side
who could share the burden with him. The
work itself needed such a companion, and
his heart cried out for such a helper.

It was this that led him to seek and find
one who was ready to share his hard life in
Rhodesia. Miss Emma Rogers, whose brother
was a Wesleyan minister in the Cape Province
of South Africa, had given her heart to Christ
and was already prepared and trained for
missionary work. There was first of all a
long and intimate correspondence and then
he went south, after she had consented to
be his wife. They were happily married at
East London, in Cape Colony, on February 3rd
1903, and came back in March to Mashonaland.

There, for nearly thirty years, they shared the work together, until in 1932 he was obliged to return to England for the last time, desperately ill.

Both at Epworth Farm and Waddilove, John's home was open to everyone who came to see him. No children of his own were granted him, but all the more on that account the children that grew up around them became like his own sons and daughters. John and his wife were called father and mother by all.

Long absences were from time to time required from John owing to the work of chairmanship, which he had reluctantly undertaken ; for it drew him away too often from the care of these, his children in the faith, at Waddilove. One journey across the Zambesi—the greatest of all—was still ahead. His absence meant for Emma, his wife, a strain of watching and waiting hard to bear. But there were also long spaces now of continuous work—teaching, guiding, helping— during which John and his wife were close together—building up the work at Waddilove. All this while the young Church was being nurtured and evangelists were being sent forth.

Accompanied by his wife, John would visit

the nearer villages. About one chief, Samuriwo, the story is told how year after year
he listened to the Gospel, till he almost knew
its story by heart ; but he could not bring
himself to obey its injunctions.

One day, when Mrs. White was present,
John asked him : " Samuriwo, when are you
going to become a Christian ? "   He replied :
" Father, I am already a Pharisee ! "

John burst out laughing at the unconscious
truth and humour of the answer. He told
Samuriwo that he must give up all his
Pharisaism and become humble as a little
child if he would enter the Kingdom of God.
But Samuriwo, like the rich young man in
the Gospel, went away sorrowful, for he had
great possessions.

Some time later Mrs. White was seriously
ill with malarial fever, and the word went
round the villages that she was about to die.
Samuriwo had halted at the mission for the
night, but hearing that the mother was very
ill, he and his carriers left immediately. So
strong was his fear of witchcraft, which is
always associated with death, that he would
not stay a moment.

But the few Christians who were gathered
at that time at the mission station spent the
night in prayer, and the women went to pray

at her bedside. Perfect love had cast out fear. The love of Jesus had taken away all the old pagan superstition.

In Africa the redemption wrought by Christ is felt most of all in the deliverance from superstitious fear of evil spirits. This makes the African Christian free with the liberty wherewith Christ has freed him. Especially from African women a heavy burden has been lifted. In Mrs. White's Bible Classes, both at Epworth and Waddilove, this wonderful realease from fear was witnessed, and it resulted in a corresponding devotion of love to the Redeemer.

A delightful account of the home life at Waddilove has been preserved to us by Morley Wright. " John White," he tells us, " impressed me at once as a man with a tremendous sense of humour. The secret of his loveableness is to be found in his humour. Though I disagreed with him on minor matters, I could not but be drawn towards him.

" In his own home he was found at his best. A better host I never expect to meet. Always cheerful, he was buoyant at the head of his heavily-laden table. How his infectious laugh used to set us all at ease as he recounted one of his most amusing anecdotes!

There seemed to be no limit to his fund of stories.

" On these occasions Mrs. White was the perfect hostess, and most obviously delighted by the merriment produced by the one she loved so dearly. The members of the staff, at these weekly dinners, were drawn together closer than at any other time. Those were indeed days to be remembered !

" And how John loved his game of billiards ! In those days the whole staff, including Mrs. White, used to try their prowess on the billiard table, but none enjoyed the game more than the Principal. Once again the infectious laugh would fill the room as some unexpected shot came off.

" On rarer occasions John White would recall the early days in Rhodesia. He would hold his guests enthralled as he told stories of the old days of adventure. As we listened, how could we help loving the ' governor ' with his merry, bespectacled face ? Modesty was always with him. Often we had to thank Mrs. White for some of the stories that showed his part in the building of the early church in Rhodesia."

A tribute to Mrs. White is paid in a farewell address which the Mashona Christians gave at their departure : " We cannot forget to mention our dear mother, Mrs. White, who has been Baba White's right hand in all his work in this country. In the hours of criticism and misunderstanding she has been a great comforter to him. Mrs. White's work among the women will be always remembered, especially at Waddilove, where it will never be cancelled. We associate ourselves with her in these times of our father's illness. We believe that God knows what is best for them. They were great missionaries and disciples of Jesus Christ."

This last sentence, written from the depth of the heart, is a noble testimony. No one could receive from African Christians a more impressive witness than that !

Many stories are told about John White's practical common sense which the Mashona will long remember. Once a new village was to be formed near to Waddilove ; but a leading Christian, called Shamu, wanted it to be called by his name, and Gombera wished to have his name attached to it. So they both went to John White.

" Go and build your church first," said John with a smile. So each man went back. Gombera said to his people : " If we build the church first, it will be called Gombera's Kraal," and Shamu said the same thing to

his people. The result was that the church
was built with remarkable speed between
them, each building one part of it. The two
men went back and told John that the church
was finished.

John's eyes twinkled with fun as he bade
them take the next step. " Go and tell your
people," he said, " both of you, that I shall be
there next Sunday to open the church ; and at
the end of the service I will tell you the name ! "

On the following Sunday a great congregation had gathered, and they eagerly awaited
the end of the service.

" The name of the church," said John, " is
' Border Church,' because it is built on the
border, between Waddilove Farm and the
Reserve."

Thus the rivalry between the two was
ended. Both were satisfied, and all the
villagers enjoyed the humour of John White's
practical decision. The church is called
" Border Church " to this day.

On another occasion Shamu wanted to get
married. He wished the marriage to take
place at a village some miles away. The
father of Shamu paid the small fee in advance,
which was only charged when the marriage
was conducted at a distance and not in
Waddilove itself.

John arrived at the village, but found no bride and bridegroom ; for the father of the bride had objected to the place of the wedding and had kept back his daughter. So Shamu had to go over to his father-in-law's village. He left word for John to follow him there.

But John said : " I must teach them the value of an agreement." So he quietly went home to Waddilove without saying a word about it.

Before the day was over the bride and bridegroom and all the relatives came hurriedly over to Waddilove and asked John to perform the marriage there. This he did, and handed them back the small fee, because they had been married at Waddilove, where no fee was charged.

A friend said to John : " But who is going to pay you for all the petrol you have used in travelling out to the village and back again ? "

Said John with a smile : " But who is going to pay *them* for all the trouble *they* had to take ? "

Thus everything ended happily and John's saying was often noted with great appreciation.

In all these matters the Mashona understood John, and he was able to teach them.

Narratives about things like these would go all round the country-side and everyone would talk about them.

In the same manner each act he performed on their behalf was recounted in the village and passed into a proverb.

Morley Wright tells us how in the pulpit he had often heard John say how much he admired the African custom of quick forgiveness. John himself had the same quality. He was modest, humble and forgiving. His most bitter enemy was always received with the utmost hospitality. John continually endured wrongs done to him without a murmur, living up to the command of Christ, " Love your enemies."

But perhaps the Mashona people loved John most of all because of his wonderful patience with them at all times. He understood at once when they suffered and he suffered with them. For example, the wife of Isaac died in childbirth and there was no one to look after the child. John saw the father's great distress and said to him, " Do not fear." So John called him to live close to his own house and made provision for the care of the baby.

" I remember," Isaac said, " how Mr. and Mrs. White used to call me in from my work

and ask me to join in their family prayers.
Those prayers made all the difference to me
when my wife died, leaving me with the
baby. I had lost all hope. But Baba White
saw my trouble, and his love and his prayers
saved me. At last I became an evangelist."

Of all the tributes paid to John White,
that of Simon Chihota is perhaps the most
deeply moving :

"We trust him so much," Simon Chihota
writes, "that we take everything of ours to
him. In our mind he is a great missionary
and a good model of a Christian. He always
has time for the humblest of our people and
he never shows signs of this troubling him.
There is a little bell at the door of his office
which those who come with their troubles
ring to announce their presence. When this
bell is rung he comes to the door so promptly
that one would think he comes to meet a
king. The bell rings so often, day and night,
that even the most humble man of any colour
would be annoyed ; but not so Baba White.
No one is too low for him to shake hands
with."

Christ in His parable of Judgment has
declared that His followers can see Himself
in those who are sick and in prison and in
distress. John saw in the humblest Mashona

the vision of the Saviour. He came to the door when the knock was heard, "to meet a King." The King was Christ.

The same presence of the Lord Jesus in one who was sick may be traced in the following story which John tells :

"I was passing," he relates, "through a village when the people told me that there was a poor woman who was very sick.

"The sight which I saw was terribly shocking. The poor woman lay in a hut, with her arm in the last stages of putrefaction. Nothing whatever had been done to remedy the evil. The story they told me was that she had been bitten by another woman.

"What was to be done ? They were entirely without medical aid to meet a case like this. The only thing was to get her consent to go to the hospital at Salisbury, forty miles away, for an operation. We managed to get her to agree, and I took her to the hospital.

"The operation was successful, and when I went to see her ten days later she was full of smiles and gratitude."

The same thing happened with a poor man whose whole leg had festered. John was able to have him removed and the leg amputated just in time to save his life. Out of that one act of tender kindness the whole district round began to seek for teachers who should tell them the Gospel of the Love of Christ.

Morley Wright gives a picture of John White on his travels which brings him very near to us indeed.

" Hundreds of miles," he writes, " I have driven John White over the rough roads of the Reserve. Wherever he went the people all knew him, and he knew them and called them by name. Not as a visitor did he arrive in a village, but as a member of the village coming home. His smile and cheery word brought joy to the hearts of all.

" It was most unusual for us to leave a village without some teeth extractions. How patient they all were ! I remember one poor woman being held down by the others while the extraction proceeded. On one occasion we were stopped by an old woman in agony from toothache. We had forgotten the forceps that day. John White explained to the woman, but she would not be appeased. As a last resort he took the pliers from the car and successfully removed the tooth, which happened to be loose.

" One night we slept at a village called Masikana. We had to spend the night in the mud church, because it had come on to

rain. Before retiring John read his New
Testament by the light of a lantern. I
wondered what would be his procedure for
prayers. After undressing and before getting
between the blankets, there he kneeled and
bowed his head. I felt humbled to see the
laughing, light-hearted veteran calmly kneeling there on his blankets saying his prayers.
Sincerity of purpose marked his whole life."

CHAPTER X : WORSE THAN SLAVERY

THERE are sometimes to be met with men and women who become such ardent champions of the cause they represent that they lose all sense of proportion and are merely partisans. In their intense zeal they seem able to see nothing but good in the cause they are advocating, and nothing but evil in the arguments of those who oppose them.

John's irresistible fund of humour, breaking out on the most unlikely occasions, saved him from any danger of partisanship of that kind, even on behalf of those he loved most in the world—the village Africans who lived in the kraals around him. He could always enjoy a laugh, especially at his own expense, and he was far too humble a man not to sense from afar the danger of " self " coming in and spoiling a good cause. Those who knew him well realised that he was diffident to a fault. Only with the greatest effort could he bring himself to court publicity, leading on to notoriety, on any subject on which he felt deeply. He would do everything in his power, first of all, to get the matter settled by personal interview without any public representation.

In the same way, while he spoke out in the very strongest manner, as a last resort, against the wrong done by Europeans to Africans, he was equally outspoken in his condemnation of the *social* wrongs that were committed by Africans themselves in their own kraals. Nothing roused his moral indignation more than the inhuman treatment of the young girls which went on, unchecked, all around him.

Quite early in his career he exposed, in flaming language, the child-slavery of these young girls, who were sold by their fathers in marriage without any choice of their own, but, on the contrary, with every mark of barbarous cruelty if they ever dared to refuse what had been decided for them.

" These degraded people," he wrote concerning the Mashona villagers, " owing to one of their cherished customs, deny to their women one of the most sacred prerogatives of their sex—the right of decision in their own marriage arrangements. Through several painful cases, brought to my notice of late, the cruelty and wickedness of this system has been forced on my very attention as never before.

" The custom is for the men concerned to arrange the terms of purchase for a girl while she is yet a mere child, sometimes a babe in arms. The girl is handed over by her father, when the terms of the contract are fulfilled and she has reached the usual age for marrying.

" But throughout the whole transaction no recognition whatever is made of her preference or wishes. She is a mere chattel in their hands. Neither is any consideration paid for disparity of age.

" A man of sixty will compel a girl scarcely a third of his own age to marry him. When a man having a number of wives dies, these are handed over to a younger brother, or the eldest son, who disposes of them as he deems best.

" A girl who recently refused to marry a man, and came to us for protection, told us that the man whom she was to marry was then the husband of her own aunt. It is easy to understand from this how degrading the custom is for the men themselves. All the finest human feelings seem buried in them. But it is the cruelty of the system on the women that I wish to make clear."

John then explains how, when the time of marriage arrives, the majority of the women sullenly and doggedly submit to the arrangement. The custom of generations, and their own helplessness, seem to have crushed every sentiment of independence in them and to have led them to believe that they were born to such servitude. But in exceptional cases they may resist this brutality of being forced to live with a man whom they loathe, and the girl will then refuse to obey her father.

If this ever happens there is an immediate resentment among the men of the kraal and a determination to break her independence. In order to reduce her to submission they inflict incredible barbarities. One of their methods is to fasten her to the ground and make a fire sufficiently near to madden her with pain without killing her. Should she, in her frenzy, promise at last to comply with their wishes, she is sent direct to her savage purchaser. Other tortures, even more revolting, are sometimes practised if her refusal continues unbroken.

In some instances the poor girl, in utter despair, will run away or commit suicide.

" Only the other day," John writes, " one of the girls told me that rather than marry the man who had bought her, she would kill herself. We were able to intercede in the matter, and in spite of the hostility of the chief and his head man, I married her to the man she desired."

John goes on to explain the extraordinary difficulty that presents itself when girls who attend Christian schools begin to realise their own personal rights and duties and refuse to be bought and sold in this slavish manner.

"Why," they ask, "should we leave our own village, with its Christian teacher, where we are each day learning about God who loves us, and go to a man we do not want to marry and live in a village where we will no longer be taught about God, or go to the House of Prayer ? "

John tells, in conclusion, a fine story about that great hero, John Molele, who took one of these girls under his care and brought her up as a true Christian. While Molele was still living, she was safe and happy and full of joy in her Christian faith, and Molele offered her his protection. But when the Mashona Rebellion broke out and Molele was murdered,[1] she came again under the cruel power of her persecutors.

"Two months ago," writes John White, " I saw her again, but she was so changed and miserable-looking that I hardly recognised her. Even before she had told me her sad tale I guessed what had taken place."

When she declared to John White that she

[1] See chapter V, p. 46.

was determined to run away from her brutal husband, he did not dissuade her. And when she had escaped, he protected her and placed her in the home of one of his evangelists, where she was able to remain in safety.

John's chivalry, mingled with indignation that could hardly be restrained, made it difficult for him ever to submit to such things as these going on before his eyes without attempting a rescue. Only the affection which he had won far and wide among the Mashona people enabled him to do daring things, to break down this evil custom, without rousing bitter hatred and resentment. Even the Government could hardly countenance now and then some rescue work which he had accomplished by the sheer moral weight of his personality and his universal repute as a " man of God." He would bring the most flagrant cases to the notice of Government, but the authorities hesitated to act.

" Only the grace of God," he writes, " can successfully remedy these evils and eradicate such savage instincts from the human heart. All other help is vain. At some of our mission stations, where the Gospel has taken a deep hold of the people, we find this whole system, that is worse than slavery, entirely disappearing. All its attendant evils are vanishing with it."

While, therefore, John White never spared his own people and dealt outright with unmitigated evil, wherever he saw it active in cruelty and brutality, he recognised at the same time that ignorance was at the root rather than deliberate wickedness. On the other hand, the cruelty which was not seldom practised by Europeans, though based on ignorance also, was due to a *culpable* ignorance; for those who practised it were Christians, who had been brought up in Christian homes.

John would refer again and again to Christ's solemn warning about the servant who knew the Master's will :

" And that servant which knew his lord's will and prepared not himself, neither did his lord's will, shall be beaten with many stripes. But he that knew not and did commit things worthy of stripes shall be beaten with few stripes. For unto whomsoever much is given, of him shall much be required, and to whom men have committed much, of him they will ask the more."[1]

These ignorant Mashona people, John would say, who have never yet had the full light of

[1] Luke xii, 47, 48.

the Gospel which has been committed to us,
deserve infinite pity even when one sternly
rebukes them for what they must know, in
their heart of hearts, to be evil. But those
who have had the full light of Christian love
in their own homes and yet are cruel towards
those over whom they rule, are in danger of
sinning *against* the light, and that is a far
more grievous offence in the sight of Him
Who is no respecter of persons, but judges
every man with equal justice.

ONE of the dearest friends John ever had was
Arthur Shearly Cripps, the poet and missionary, who loves both Oxford and Mashonaland with a rare and deep affection. He has
enshrined this love in beautiful English verse.
Some of his songs are likely to live on when
other things mentioned in this book have
been forgotten. They have already found a
place in the anthologies of English modern
verse.

Three things, above all else, endeared him
to John White. The first was his pure
devotion to his Lord and Master, Jesus Christ,
Whom he loved and served, as King of Love,
with all his soul. The second was his simple
Franciscan life, lived in the utmost poverty
in the heart of Mashonaland. The third was
his fearless championship of the African in
face of bitter contumely. " Blessed are those
who are persecuted for righteousness' sake,"
said Jesus, " for theirs is the Kingdom of
Heaven." John felt that Arthur, more than
any other friend he had, was an inheritor of
that blessing. For he had stood out even

against his own countrymen on behalf of the
rights of the Mashona people.

At one period, when Arthur Cripps and
John White were fighting valiantly together
side by side in order to save for the Wanjanja
tribes the Sabi Reserve intact, and also other
areas which were threatened, Arthur, with
his poet's vision, had seen the blue and
emerald hills of the Reserve, like the jewels
that shone on Aaron's breastplate, as remem-
brancers of the tribes of Israel.   He wrote:

> *Aaron's breastplate held a few*
> *Flashing jewels o'er his heart.*
> *Graved was each gem's emblem due*
> *With some tribe's beloved name. . . .*

He turns to the tribes of the Wanjanja in
the Sabi Reserve:

> *A remembrancer I wear,*
> *Near my heart, in work or sleep.*
> *'Tis my view and vision clear*
> *Of those hills,—as yesterday,—*
> *Standing blue about my way.*
> *Near my heart, their gems I keep*
> *Sparkling fresh in sunlight's flames,—*
> *Near my heart, the wild tribes' names,*
> *In their granite, graven deep.*

John used continually to urge his poet

friend to be more simple. His own taste was modelled on Wordsworth's poems written among his own Cumberland dales. He wished all poetry to be simple and direct like those. But Arthur Cripps could no more change his style and make it less mystical than a leopard could change his spots ; and he has gone on writing his own rare English verse,—not seldom concerning his friend, John White, himself.

Arthur is now well over sixty years of age, but he still preserves his wonderful physical fitness under the hardest conditions of living, which would be quite impossible for ordinary Europeans to endure. Year in, year out, he lives as closely as possible to the African mode of life, in all its simplicity, dwelling in an African hut and eating the simple food which Africans usually eat. With an inner joy and peace, he brings happiness out of every discomfort, because it is all undertaken for the sake of Him, " Who, though He was rich, yet for our sakes became poor."[1]

With John White, during his illness at Kingsmead Close, the one unfailing pleasure that came to him, week after week, was Arthur's letter from Mashonaland, always with some intimate touch of news in it about the

[1] 2 Cor. viii, 9.

Mashona people and some message of love from the writer.

In return, the one duty that John never missed, however much pain he might be suffering, was to reply in his own handwriting to his friend. He used to call this his " love letter " ; and when his friend's letter came from Rhodesia he would hold it up in triumph and a gleam of light would sparkle in his eyes as he said to me, " Here's another letter from Arthur. He never forgets."

The poet's handwriting was almost impossible to decipher, and John would say with a laugh : " Charlie, did you ever see such a scrawl ? Why, it's worse than a schoolboy's ! "

The letters also had a troublesome way of wandering over every odd corner of the sheet of paper on which they were written, and this would also cause great amusement.

What follows was dictated by John concerning his friend from his sick-room as a final testimony. It needs to be recorded in full :

" When the annals of Rhodesia are faithfully recorded, and the personalities who have influenced the country most potently and beneficially are written, the Rev. Arthur Shearly Cripps will occupy a very high place.

At present no one appreciates the true value
of the service he is rendering. Colonists look
upon him as a strange and eccentric man,
whose teaching and treatment of the natives
is doing a great deal to spoil them. For his
character they have the highest regard, but
think nothing of his judgment in matters of
this kind. By them he is entirely misunderstood.

" A clergyman of the Church of England,
he came to Rhodesia over twenty years ago,
and settled down to the work of an ordinary
missionary. But he came to see that the
things required of him by his Church and by
the Government might hinder his truest work
and his testimony. The mission schools
received grants from the Government to
assist in education ; these he refused on the
ground that they gave the Government too
much say in the conduct of his schools.

" Gradually his attitude to his own Church
changed a good deal, and he felt that he could
not be bound by its regulations. And so
from the S.P.G. he turned away somewhat,
and does not now receive a licence from the
Bishop of the Diocese. But what the colonists think about him and his connection
with the Church are very small matters to
him. He has got a generous soul. All the

denominations are his friends; he preaches the Gospel wherever opportunity is offered him.

" On the social side of his life Cripps is a champion for better treatment and kinder relations between the races. He lives almost as they live, on the very simplest food and in a hut similar to those that the Africans themselves occupy. Indeed, poverty seems to be his motto. And so he comes near to those people, and they can see in him a true representative of the Christ who dwelt on the earth amongst us. If he hears of a Mashona sick twenty miles away, he will take his blanket on his shoulders and march off to see him, sometimes doing the journey in a single day. He is always urging upon the Government to give more medical help to the needy African people. On this ground alone he is greatly beloved.

" He watches their cases in the Law Courts. If there is a miscarriage of justice, he is the man to point this out. If there is ill-treatment by the white man of his black servants, Cripps takes an interest in stopping this. When the Land question was before the country, he was the leader and agitator for a more ample provision of land on the Reserves for the Mashona. He wrote pamphlets, he interviewed Government officials, he represented the case in England, and did everything possible to get an increase of the acreage.

"His fight over the Juvenile Act, which proposed to indenture young boys, was a strenuous one, and in the end proved successful. He stood up in the Missionary Conference, pleading with the passion and pathos of one of the old Hebrew prophets, that there should be no restriction imposed upon any African whom God had called to preach the Gospel. In this case he succeeded.

"For twenty years this man has honoured and blessed me by his friendship. Its value has not been merely sentimental, though I love him as a man. But he has set before me a high ideal. His frequent letters have reminded me of tasks to face and urged me to toil on. Few of us who know him can walk in his steps ; we tread falteringly in the way that he blazed. He is our modern St. Francis of Assisi—in many respects a worthy successor of that great Saint.

"Amongst the scattered white population he does a work that is having its effect in bringing these people to a knowledge of God and benefiting their lives generally. Two of his friends at different periods were in the Salisbury Hospital, over a hundred miles away. To see these he made the trip on foot, no roof covered him at night; he slept under the open sky. To help any friend in trouble he would yield the last coin he possessed. His feats of walking are the talk of his district; though now over sixty years of age, he does twenty, and sometimes thirty, miles each day, partaking of very little food and sleeping at night under the most uncomfortable conditions. Bodily comforts and the things that men are careful of he scarcely regards.

"This is the man who has influenced me more than any other in Rhodesia for the last twenty-five years."

In all that follows later concerning John White's wider influence as the outstanding personality in Southern Rhodesia, who would never allow any public act to be done there, adversely affecting the African, without a protest, it must be borne in mind that Arthur Cripps was always by his side and their names were linked together both in the public press and in the public mind. Without this loyal help from such an unimpeachable soul John White's own influence would have carried far less weight. Like David and Jonathan they were undivided, both in their love for one another and in their public service.

Just as John has written down with great deliberation his own witness concerning his friend, so Arthur has given his testimony concerning John. The following passages, taken from it, will make clear, in a poet's language, what Arthur thought of John White.

" When John returned to England in 1928," Arthur Cripps writes, " he was newly come from much uphill crusading on behalf of the Africans. . . . He sailed again, not long after, for his old sentinel's post in the firing-line. 'Eternal vigilance is the price of liberty,' was his maxim.

" When I came back to Africa, in 1930, I made straight for his home at Maswingo. He was no longer the Governor of a great institution, but had pastoral work and the training of some candidates for the ministry and Bible study. He came out to our Sunrise Mission, and spoke very nobly to our African congregation, comparing the trouble, which the older Christians had with the younger generation, to the trouble which our Heavenly Father has with us.

" He lives in the eternal love of God, but he lives also in the earthly lives of us whom he taught to ' seek first the Kingdom of God and His righteousness.' What

Christian ever touched the heart of pagan
Africa as he did ?

" His love to me was that 'something to
love,' whereof it is written,

> *God gives us love.   Something to love*
> *He lends us.   But when love is grown*
> *To ripeness, that on which it throve*
> *Falls off, and love is left alone.*

" Sturdily English by birth, but African
by adoption, he chose to be buried among
Africans. Having loved Africa—he loved her
to the end.

" ' Certain men slept upon a plain,' wrote
Olive Schreiner, ' and the night was chill and
dark. And, as they slept, at that hour when
night is darkest, one stirred.

" ' Far off to the eastward, through his
half-closed eyes he saw, as it were, one faint
line, thin as a hair's breadth, that edged the
hill-tops ; and he whispered in the darkness
to his followers : " The dawn is coming."

" ' But they with fast-closed eyelids, mur-
mured, " He lies. There is no dawn."

" ' Nevertheless, Day broke.'

" John told me," Arthur Cripps ends,
" how he was planning to leave the where-
withal to found a Hospital in his own beloved

district in Mashonaland. In his own suffering, he had been learning how worth while it was to do something to help those who suffered. God surely has called him, as His friend, to come up higher—higher both in courage and compassion."

Other extracts will be taken from Arthur Cripps's articles which he wrote to me week after week after the death of his friend. That which I have here quoted gives the true vision of John White as he saw him with the eye of faith.

CHAPTER XII : THE ZAMBESI AT LAST

THE one longing of John's heart, through all the years of patient waiting in Mashonaland, had been to press forward towards the north, where the great River Zambesi divided Central Africa on the east, and the still greater River Congo divided it on the west. But no opportunity had been given him hitherto. More than once, his own health had given way and he had been invalided home. In the years 1912 and 1913 it seemed as if he would be obliged to give up altogether. There were also many urgent duties to be performed as Chairman of the District which did not seem to allow of any long absence.

At last, in the year 1907, an opportunity suddenly occurred. He had gone to Zwimba, the mission station which was farthest north. There the news was brought him that hundreds of villages in the Zambesi Valley were unreached as yet by any missionary at all. The opportunity of seeing things for himself was presented to him, and he took a sudden resolution, guided, as he firmly believed, by the Holy Spirit of God. After long and earnest prayer his plans were made.

He would go entirely alone and travel light. In this way he hoped to meet with no delays and be able to bring back a personal report about the possibilities of an advance. The Rev. A. Walton, who was stationed at Zwimba, was eager to go with him. But he had recently suffered severely from malaria and was still weak. John decided, therefore, only to take him for the first stages of the march. Beyond Mbowi, where they halted for a few days, John went on alone, over a rough and dangerous road, with as few carriers as possible and as quickly as they were able to travel. For speed was necessary.

" Again and again," he wrote afterwards, " I was impressed with the good Providence of God and the constant care of the Master in Whose service we were engaged. Dangers there were on every side, but we suffered no hurt. Our food supply was very precarious, but we never lacked a meal."

This rough country was the home of the lion and the hyena. It was necessary each night to build a circular fence and keep the fire alight as a protection against the wild beasts. One night, being near a kraal, John told the carriers that they need not make

the usual protective fence ; but at midnight
he was awakened by a wild yell. Looking
up, he saw to his horror a big hyena close
to the man on the outside of the group, and
another hyena close to himself. The yells,
however, had been enough to frighten them.
The two hyenas that had advanced nearer
than the rest slunk away to the whole pack,
and kept up their howls all night, making
further sleep impossible. In the morning,
they found the fresh spoors of a lion, which
had also been prowling round during the
night.

They passed now through a barren, un-
inhabited country, and then at last reached
a fertile valley where many villages were seen.
The grey-headed chief was friendly and
asked John whether he had come in search
of gold or trade.

" No," said John, " I am not a trader or
a seeker after gold. I seek other treasures.
For I have been sent by God to help you to
find the greatest treasure of all."

" But we are ignorant," said the old chief,
" and cannot be taught. What do we know
about God ? "

" Who sends you the rain ? " asked John.
" Who makes the corn to grow, and gives
you eyes to see with ? "

" We call Him Mwari," said the chief ;
" but what do *you* know about Him ? "

" He is the Heavenly Father Who loves
your people and mine also," said John.
" And I can tell you all about His love and
also where your spirit goes to when you die."

The old chief was deeply impressed. All
round him were degradation, hopelessness,
ignorance, despair. " We are filth," the chief
had said. " How can we understand ? "

John's heart was deeply touched. He had
never before seen human beings sunk so low
as these tribes.

" As I pondered on all these things," he
wrote in his diary, " F. W. H. Myers's lines
kept coming back to me :

Only like souls, I see the folk thereunder,
   Bound, who should conquer ; slaves, who
     should be kings ;
Hearing their one Hope with an empty wonder,
   Sadly contented with a show of things.

Then with a rush, the intolerable craving,
   Shivers throughout me as a trumpet call.
Oh, to save these ! To perish for their saving !
   Die for their life, be offered for them all !

After the experience of the deadly heat in

the valley, they had to pass again through
an arid region. They tramped on without
a sign of water. At last some men met
them who were coming down from the
north. These men told them that if they
left the road for a short distance and followed
a certain track, they would find a little water.
They found a small supply, which was very
precious.

Then, at last, through a gap in the hills
they looked down on the Zambesi Valley.
But there was as yet no signs of the river
itself. The great fertility of the valley showed
that the wide waters could not be far distant.
In the villages below, the orgies of beer
drinking and dancing were going on, day
after day, as they passed through. The
nights, too, were made hideous by the wild
debauchery.

"I could not help wondering," wrote
John, "how long the time would be before
these hideous orgies would give place to the
quiet sanctuary of God. May He hasten the
day!"

They found the valley to be about thirty-
five miles across. There were forests of
graceful palm trees, forty feet or more in
height. The climate was exceedingly hot
and unhealthy, quite unfit for Europeans to

live in. Villages were dotted everywhere about.

" The people," John wrote, " are in a very degraded state. Drunkenness and immorality are their predominant vices. Their ignorance is wellnigh inconceivable. St. Paul's description of the heathen world of his day would befit this region. What a task is here ! Who is equal to it ? No human device can help them ! The only Gospel that can uplift them is Christ's."

John had with him a small box of medicines. He found the children suffering from a malignant type of ophthalmia. He did so much good, even with his simple remedies, that the people begged him to stay longer in order to heal their sick.

But he had nearly reached his goal. Another march, and at last the Zambesi was reached ! As he stood on the banks of this mighty river, he lifted up his heart in thankfulness to God and tears filled his eyes. The longing of a lifetime had been accomplished !

" It is now," he wrote, " over three-quarters of a century since the first Methodist missionary landed in Cape Colony. During these eighty years a great and blessed work has been done. Many of the leaders, good

and brave men, have passed away, and their
names are wellnigh forgotten. But their
work, an imperishable monument of their
name, remains. Their unwearying toil has
made it possible for us to advance to-day
and preach the Gospel to tribes which were
in their day unknown."

The Zambesi at this point presented to
the gaze of the travellers a beautiful stretch
of water, about a mile wide. The method
of crossing it was in a dug-out, and they
accomplished the crossing in safety. Time,
however, would not allow John either to
stay or to go farther. The utmost limit of
absence had been reached. He had already
been eight weeks on the march and there
was still the return journey to accomplish.

John nearly lost his life just after they
had crossed the river Zambesi on their way
back. One of the carriers had badly injured
his toe, and John was kneeling down to bind
up the wound. He reached behind to his
hip pocket to get his clasp knife, but instead
of his hand closing round the hilt of the knife,
it caught hold of a deadly snake which had
slithered down a tree. John flung the snake
from him with a sudden start. His dog
dashed forward at the snake and received
its fangs in his neck. In half an hour, in

spite of all John could do to check the poison
from spreading, the dog's head and neck had
swollen to double the size, and it was some
days before the poor animal fully recovered.
The poison was very nearly fatal.

No one could have put the results of this
amazing journey more modestly than John
himself did on his return.

" Its importance," he wrote, " must not
be over estimated. As far as real effective
work goes, it counted for little. Before the
army of the Church of Christ has won the
territory where I have been, and stands
victorious where I stood, long years of self-
sacrificing toil will have to be endured, yea,
and—it may be true !—blood shed. But if
we are true to the purpose of the Master and
the genius of our Church, advance we must."

" THE incident," says John, " which in the Providence of God brought us beyond the Zambesi into Central Africa, is full of romance. The story reads like a novel.

" A youth had come from the Luano Valley, two hundred miles north of the Zambesi River, to work in Southern Rhodesia. He went to labour on a mine, attended one of our little churches, and there came to know Christ, the world's Saviour. Returning, he told his father, a chief, of his discovery. The old man was much impressed, and urged his son to go back and see if he could induce a missionary to come to his country to teach his people.

" Before the son started on this quest, the old man died. When the son was thus raised to the position of Chief, he desired for himself and his people Christian teaching, and determined to make the journey back to Southern Rhodesia in search of it.

" One day, four years ago, with a few attendants, he arrived at Epworth, having walked 350 miles. His story and his earnest appeal greatly impressed me, as a call from God ; and yet I knew not how to respond to it at that time.   How could I be absent for two months on a trip into the interior ?

" I said to the young man, ' You can rest here for a day or two and I will give you my answer.'

" My wife and I made this a matter of prayer and we talked it over.   To her, it meant six or eight weeks of loneliness, but in the end she said, ' You must go with this man, and I will do the best I can in your absence.' "

One request touched them all at Epworth very much.   Chikara, the young chief, said that he found it very difficult to convince his tribe that Jesus Christ lived.   He was sure, however, that they would be convinced if they could see a picture of Him.   Strangely enough, John had no picture.   He told Chikara that the purity of his own life would be a better testimony to Jesus than any picture.

Two months later, John left the rail-head in Northern Rhodesia and walked 150 miles inland into Chikara's country.   No missionary had ever visited this region before and they were eager to have evangelists to teach them.

After the way had thus been opened, John appealed to the Church at home. One Christian in South Africa offered £500 and one in England offered £1,000. So the work was started.

The Rev. J. H. Loveless and John White, with three evangelists, then started on the main journey. They would have to interview chiefs, select a mission station and make all necessary arrangements.

The heat of the Zambesi Valley was terrific. They could only travel in the early morning and late afternoon.

"We made our way," John writes, "through the thick undergrowth that tore the skin on our arms and legs and made progress slow and difficult. Night was often made hideous by the roar of lions and the growl of leopards.

"For two nights we had slept close to a river, where savage mosquitoes made sleep impossible. I never remember, in all my long experience, being attacked in such a persistent and effectual manner. We arrived on the third night on an elevated position near a kraal. Here, we thought, we should have a good night's rest. We made the usual fires, but took no other precaution. Our meal finished, we lay down. Soon my companion was sound asleep, but I lay awake for a time.

"Far away, I could hear the loud, unearthly roar of a lion, and farther still, another responded. 'This is a nice business,' I thought to myself. 'We escape the mosquitoes to be disturbed by lions.' In a few minutes it roared again and the other responded—much nearer.

"Nearer and nearer it came, till I deemed it advisable to wake the sleeping camp. We gathered ourselves into a compact group— four of us with guns ready, and the carriers all with assegais in their hands. Afraid lest someone should, in the excitement, fire before we were ready, I gave orders that none should fire until I gave the word. There, kneeling in suspense, peering into darkness, we waited quite five minutes without hearing a sound.

"Then, at what seemed like thirty yards distance, there came the most terrible roar I have ever heard.

"As soon as my voice could be heard above the noise I called 'Fire' and in a moment three of us fired at the spot where we thought our visitor stood. Not a further sound was heard.

"In the morning, we looked for the spoor

and there at about three lions' bounds distance we saw the spot where the lion had
sprung away after we had fired. Enquiring
in the morning from the people in the kraal
we found that the lion had come into their
midst the night before and, in spite of noise
and firing their blunderbusses, had refused to
go away."

As they went on, the track became very
difficult. On the highland the cold at night
was very great. At one place, they were
met by a friendly headman, Mwanabunga,
who offered to go with them and guide them
through the unknown country.

Now the track descended into a valley of
dense undergrowth where the heat became
more and more unbearable. " It was the
hottest place," says John White, " that I
have ever known. One day, the heat nearly
killed me. So overcome was I, that at one
point, like Jonah, I prayed that God would
take away my life."

Food was now getting scarce. So one
morning John set out after some guinea fowl,
with his gun, alone. He followed the birds
until the sun was high and he knew it was
time to get back.

Then he suddenly discovered he was
lost ! He tried to get his bearings by some

landmark, but nothing was to be seen which could show him the way. He shouted and fired his gun, but there was no reply. Then he stopped still, in order to get the right direction and so regain the path. The undergrowth was dense ; the heat was beginning to be intolerable. His thirst was becoming greater every moment—and he knew he was lost !

He fired off several shots, but again there was no reply. The horror of that moment, when the certainty dawned upon him that he was lost and alone in the dense jungle, can easily be imagined.

But John was not alone : for God was with him, and the momentary horror passed away. With his heart uplifted in prayer to God he went forward and took courage. Later in the afternoon he crossed a path, but there were no carriers. Then he came to a rather foul water-hole. But this was better than nothing, and cupping his hands, he dipped them into the muddy water and strained it as best as he could before raising it to his mouth.

A little later two men came along who were alarmed to see a European. John made them understand that he had lost his carriers. He promised to reward them well if they

could find them. Before very long they
returned, saying that they had found the
carriers not far away. With deep thankfulness to God he went forward and after some
time came upon them and thus was saved
from what might have meant certain
death.

" At Chikara's Kraal," John writes, " a
great disappointment awaited us.   The chief
Chikara had been killed by a wild elephant
two months before. But his people gave us
a very hearty reception. The Chief, who
succeeded him, an elderly man named Mbosha,
showed us much kindness, giving us food for
ourselves and our porters. He told us that
Chikara, in spite of his people's taunts, held
to the belief that I would eventually return
and that his people would have the Gospel
preached unto them.

" While I was there, quite a unique opportunity presented itself of explaining our
mission. A mourning ceremony, on account
of the death of Chikara the Chief, was being
gone through. Providentially, I think, our
visit coincided with this ceremony ; for,
from far and near, those men and their
families had gathered. During a sober in-
terval, I collected them and explained in
detail the meaning of our visit. I reminded

them that Chikara possessed knowledge that we would fain give to them.

"When I had finished, one of the teachers said that the Chief Mbosha had already had some little instruction, and if I asked him he thought he would engage in prayer.

"It was a very moving and pathetic sight to see this old man first explaining to this astonished gathering what prayer meant, and then in a very childlike manner lifting up his heart to the Great Father.

"I told him our plans. We would go back and select on the plateau a healthy site for our central station. Then when the rains were over we would place teachers along the river, where the people resided. This old chief would be the first to receive one.

"The aged man said, 'Leave part of your luggage behind, so that when I look upon it I may know that you are soon returning.'

"I was greatly impressed with the eagerness everywhere of these people to hear the word of God. In all my thirty years experience, I have never seen people so apparently eager as these two tribes.

"Let me describe one scene. We had arrived at Liteta, the village of a chief. On our arrival I was told that a chief seven miles distant wished to speak to me. I sent for him, and he explained that he wished very much that I would send a teacher to his people. I had hardly made the tentative promise to do so when Liteta, the paramount chief, came along. He eagerly requested that a teacher should be sent to *his* people.

" I told him that I did not see how, with the scarcity of men, I could send two. Then he said, 'As paramount chief, I have first claim!' And I witnessed the spectacle of two chiefs arguing with high and angry words their rival claims for a Christian teacher.

" One group of men said, ' See our hair is grey and if you do not send him soon we shall be in our graves.

" We selected a site on the healthiest convenient spot we could find for a main station and started an out-station five miles away. Huts have been built for the minister and his teacher. A little mud church is already built. The other day I saw a picture of the opening—a group of sixty people standing outside, who now gather together to worship Him of whom they had not heard only a few months ago.

" Now, in the Providence of God, they are

ours to win for Christ. This is the Providential Era in Africa. May God bestir us all to take our share in fulfilling our great, imperative duty."

The Rev. J. H. Loveless took charge of this new mission station. But a very grave epidemic of smallpox broke out in the neighbourhood soon after he had taken up his station : and he gave himself night and day to helping and relieving the sick and thus endeared himself to them. When the rains came he suffered a great deal from malaria and was obliged to return for a time to England.

He came back again to Southern Rhodesia, and after a life of devoted sacrifice passed away on February 5th, 1924, at Salisbury. Few men were loved by the Africans as he was loved, and it was his joy to lay down his life in their service.

CHAPTER XIV : WADDILOVE

At rare times, in his missionary life, John had the joy of founding some institution, which was destined to become a permanent organ of the growing Christian Church in S. Rhodesia, fulfilling a function as vital to the Body of Christ as sight or touch are to the human body.

Of all the efforts made in this direction, there was none on whose upbuilding he bestowed such earnest prayer and devoted labour as Waddilove.

The story of its actual foundation has already been told in some measure. But, fortunately, John himself can carry us further in his own inimitable way by telling us incidents which come out of the very centre of his own experience. They make Waddilove live before us as a garden of young human lives blossoming into flower and bearing precious fruit. For here, often for the first time, they enter upon the higher life of the Spirit as children of the Heavenly Father. Here they learn that " first love " for Christ which is the most beautiful thing in the world, as it rises like a lotus out of the mire of the old pagan life.

In this chapter I shall quote for the most part John's own words and thus let him tell his own story. His narrative, it is true, starts at a period long after Waddilove was founded and we have to leave on one side, for a moment, the order in which things happened; but the picture of Waddilove itself stands out very clearly and we get its true proportions. The narrative carries with it also the love which was in John's heart towards this Institution.

" We often say," John writes, " and it is strangely true of every period of Church History, that the blood of the martyrs is the seed of the Christian Church. Many people have heard the name of Mr. C. E. O. Rush. I shall always thank God that I was privileged to be associated with this splendid servant of God. He had only one interest—the Kingdom of Our Lord Jesus Christ. Although he did not learn sufficient of the language to speak to the people in their own tongue, his influence upon them spiritually was wonderful. They regarded him as a man who, like Enoch, walked with God. When he passed, they said that God had taken him. So it transpired that his frail body was not equal to the demands made upon it by his ardent spirit. After eighteen months of work at the school, the disease from which he suffered reasserted itself ; he was laid aside, lingered for a time, and passed to the Master's higher service.

" It was during the vacation that he died ; so only a few were present at the funeral. When, however, the school reassembled, the students said to me, ' Our father has gone ; we could not be at the funeral ; we should like to have a service now to show our respect and affection for one who has helped us so much.'

" So on a bright morning in February, we assembled for his memorial service on the very spot at which I had stood thirty-two years before.　We sang some of the choruses he had taught them ;　' Since Jesus came into my heart,' ' Wonderful, wonderful Jesus,' and ' Never lose sight of Jesus.'　After that, we gave thanks to God for his noble ministry and asked that we might have grace to tread in his steps.　Then we returned to our work.

" Come with me in imagination to that memorial service.　Try to see—as I saw the scene and gaye thanks—the tremendous difference between this gathering and that which took place in 1896.　In this company to-day there are four hundred students. They represent the most progressive section of the people. Some may have come for more selfish motives ; but I speak now of the majority.

" Some are candidates for our Ministry ; forty are in training for our evangelistic work ; some eighty more are taking a teachers' course adapted to their attainments and the needs of the country. The balance is composed of young men and women who have come to this centre that they may receive a fuller education than is possible in their own towns or villages. Great is the African's yearning at the present moment for education.

" If you could look in the direction of the old site of Molele's hut, you would see a set of buildings that are the surprise and admiration of most of the people who visit us.

" There are two large dormitories for boys and girls respectively, a large practising school, class - rooms, workshops, houses for the staff, a hospital, and a very beautiful and commodious church. There is no debt on these buildings. We had a grant from the Centenary Fund. Sir Joshua Waddilove helped us generously, and the balance has been found by ourselves. Most of the work of building has been done by the staff and students in training.

" Looking right into the distance, we see some huge granite boulders. Near that spot lives the chief, Chizhengeni. It was this chief and his people who were responsible for the death of Molele and James White, the settler, during the rebellion. Three years ago these people came to me and asked that they might have a teacher sent to their settlement. I was able to comply. So it transpires that the descendants and friends of these murderers have now their own Church, School and Society Class. Towards our missionary funds they last year contributed.

" What is it we are seeking to do for this family of four hundred that has been committed to us ?

" As far as our resources allow, we are trying to open every door of opportunity they are capable of entering. In this enterprise we get very generous assistance from the Government. You would see shops for carpentry, a spinning and weaving school for the girls. We make our own bricks, and the buildings are erected by our own people. We have a large farm, on which we teach better methods of agriculture and grow most of the food we require. Every student is required to do two and a half hours of manual work each day. From six o'clock in the morning until six in the evening it is a veritable hive of industry.

" All of our people are very keen on scholastic work ; if you want to punish one of the scholars, it is only necessary to tell him that he must not go to school. We have a Practising School, in which those who are to be teachers receive lessons in the art of teaching.

" In the centre of the compound stands the church—the House of God : all the other buildings cluster round it. This is symbolic of our ideal. We aim at giving Christ the central place in all our lives. If we fail to make disciples of Christ of these people, then we have missed the mark.

" Civilisation without Christianity is a doubtful gift. Education, without the restraints and discipline of the Christian faith, may be a danger rather than a boon to these heathen people. On this side of our work we have much to cheer us.

" Come with me, if you will, to this spot on the first Sunday of the month. At seven-thirty o'clock in the morning we meet to partake of the Lord's Supper. There are about two hundred and fifty communicants.

These represent half a dozen tribes at least, and two distinct nationalities. Together we kneel, black and white, Matabele and Mashona, Basuto and Batonga—tribes that a few years ago were in deadly feud with each other. Now we are all one in Christ Jesus.

" On the other Sundays of the month we meet at seven for prayer, and generally have the Church full. At 10.30 we gather for public worship. It would do your soul good to listen to these folk singing our great Christian hymns, both in English and in their own tongue. In the afternoon everyone, irrespective of age, goes to Sunday School. Again at seven in the evening another public service is held.

" We endeavour to teach by precept and practice that Sunday is intended as a Day supremely for worship. My Society Class on Wednesday is composed of a hundred and fifty men ; Mrs. White has forty women in her Class. The younger people are in classes on trial, or Junior Society Classes. Near to the site of this Institution there is an area occupied by Africans, called a Reserve. To the villages in this area some of the students go out in bands to preach to the people. In this way we keep the evangelist students in touch with what is to be the work of their life.

" Near the Girls' Hostel you will notice another building, not large but very significant. It is the Hospital. Like the other buildings, it was erected by the students and the Staff. Our Missionary Committee gave us a third of the money, and we raised the rest ourselves. As yet we have not been able to get a doctor, but we have a trained Nurse in charge.

" There is a tremendous amount of disease and suffering among our people. They are totally ignorant of medical science or of anything approaching to first aid.

" The amateur Missionary does what he can. Professional people, I know, regard his work with disfavour ; he is supposed to do more harm than good. I don't believe it. Instead of flocking to our doors, they would have left us long ago if this had been the case. In my ministry, I have distributed scores of pounds' worth of the simpler remedies ; treated thousands of people with wounds and sores.

" But we feel that this amateur service is not enough ; it is not worthy of the Church of Him who went about doing good and healing the people's diseases. We must give of our best. So we have our Hospital and Nurse, and ere long hope to have a Doctor too.

In the short time we have been open, hundreds of people have been helped. The lives of at least three infants were saved in the first three months that we were open. In addition to this, the Nurse has six African girls in training for her own profession. What an inestimable boon these will be to their own people when they go out !

" This ministry of healing has its influence on our evangelistic work as well. Let me give you a case in point. Twenty miles away lives the paramount chief of the district, Samuriwo. He is a typical pagan. He and I have been on friendly terms for years. But he has steadily refused to allow us to put a teacher at his place or build a church there. One can understand this, for our witness would be a constant rebuke to the life he was living, with his retinue of wives and his beer drinking,

" Two years ago his young people, some forty in number, presented themselves one day at my house, desiring to speak with me. They had come to ask for a teacher. ' But,' I said, ' you cannot have one whilst your father refuses, and he objects.'

" ' We have overcome him at last,' said they with jubilation. ' We have told him that if he persists in his refusal we shall leave

him, and build our own village, where we
shall be free to do as we wish. And therefore now he has yielded.'

" So a teacher was sent to them from the
Mission centre, and was well received. Everything went well.

" About a year ago this chief got sick;
one symptom was that he lost the use of his
legs. He asked me if he might come to the
Hospital. I went across and brought him
in our Ford lorry. The rest in bed and
skilled treatment, in about six weeks, made
a great change in him; he was able to walk,
and seemed to be much better. Great was
the rejoicing of the people when I took him
back again to his village.

" A few weeks after he had returned, I went
again to the kraal to open a church that the
teacher and the people had built. We had a
brief service outside; then we opened the
door, and the congregation all marched inside. Whilst we sat for a few minutes for the
people to get composed, I noticed the people
rise in a body to welcome someone. Looking to the door, I saw the cause: the people
had risen out of respect for their chief who,
with his headman, was at the moment coming
through the door. They remained through
the service, when we dedicated this house to

the worship of God. Now it was the ulti-
matum, undoubtedly, that compelled Samuriwo to allow an evangelist to come to his
kraal, but it was the ministrations of Nurse
Dry that so softened his heart as to bring
him to the service to join us in this act of
worship.

"At last, after his age-long sleep, the
African is wide awake. Give your imagination wings, and you can see him there.
Personified, Africa is like a great giant. From
a pit of dark and evil spirits and many
abominations, he is trying to climb.

"But the sides of the pit are slippery and
steep. Around its mouth I see an interested
crowd. One gazes at his struggle with
cynical indifference; another of the baser
sort would kick him back; another hopes he
may not emerge, since he is more profitable
commercially as he is. Yet another I see
there, who looks on with eyes of pity. The
scarred hand is outstretched to help. ' Is it
nothing,' He asks, ' to all ye that pass by ? '

"But only through His own people can
He lift him up. To us this Son of Man turns,
and pointing to the struggling figure, says :
' Behold your younger brother ! He was
dead, but is alive again ; He was lost ; but
now, he is found ! ' "

CHAPTER XV: THE CONGO

WE have seen in other chapters how John himself at last pressed forward on his adventurous march beyond the Zambesi River; how he left his colleague, J. H. Loveless, to open and establish the work after he had returned.

His second friend and co-worker, J. W. Stanlake, fired by the same spirit, was eager to go still farther afield—as far as the Congo itself.

"A year ago," writes John White, "because of our lack of any further accommodation at Waddilove, I was obliged to send out a notice to different parts of the country, informing people that we could not receive any more students in our own Hostels.

"One day two young men turned up, with their fees in their hands, asking admission. I shook my head. 'No room,' I said. The poor chaps nearly wept.

"'Where have you come from?' I asked them.

"They informed me that they had heard of this School in the Belgian Congo, and had

therefore travelled nearly two thousand miles
to reach Waddilove !

" Well, an appeal like this was irresistible.
We pushed the beds a bit closer, made an
empty space, and took them in. . . . Great is
the African's yearning at the present moment
for education ! "

It will easily be understood what a deep
impression this incident made upon John
White and his colleagues. Later on, a request came to visit the Belgian Congo, where
new copper mines of vast extent were being
rapidly opened up.

Stanlake was set free to make the journey
and survey the ground. He sent a very full
report back to John White, which I have
not been able to trace. But a letter written
to his friend, Brigg, gives us an account, in
a brief compass, of the situation as he found it.

" The whole country," Stanlake writes
from the Belgian Congo, " is a huge forest,
but not dense.

" The ' Star of the Congo ' is a mine about
seven miles from Elizabethville. The smelt-
ing works are a mile and a half from the new
town. There is a fairly large European
population, including about four hundred
Britishers—a very mixed crowd. There are
probably twice that number of Belgians.

For this population there are seventy-two beer halls ! The wickedness of the place surpasses all I have ever seen. It is Hell !

"If our scientists get the upper hand of the sleeping sickness, then the Congo presents a land of great promise and infinite possibilities."

Stanlake goes on to describe how he was very well received by the Belgian Governor, who invited him to dine with him and had a long talk with him. He seemed in every way most anxious to assist, if only the Methodist Church were willing to undertake to found a Mission in the new mining district which was about to be developed. Subject to the approval of the Belgian Government, he offered Stanlake two plots of ground in the township and three farms, of a considerable acreage, on which to establish agricultural schools. Stanlake reported that he hardly expected that the Belgian Government would give them all that was offered, but the fact that they were ready to offer any site at all was itself a sign of goodwill.

The future town, in connection with the copper mine, was to be placed at Kombove, and the railway line from Elizabethville would be extended thus far. A very large number of African labourers would be employed, and this would give an extensive field for mission work.

Stanlake ends this remarkable letter with a note of caution.

" The great objection," he writes, " to the whole scheme is that we are leaving behind us over nine hundred miles of British territory, which offers great facilities for African work, and it would seem to me that our first call is here.

" If our Missionary Society decides on a big advance in the near future, then un-questionably the Congo offers a splendid field. On the other hand; if they can only send out one or two men, in that case we had better leave the Congo to the future, and do the work that lies nearest to our own doors in British territory. You have probably heard that the Committee are adverse to our going to the Congo, and I think they are right not to rush things.

" It will be a great undertaking, and unless it is done on a fairly big scale, it is better left undone. Our love to you."

When the whole question had been fully considered by the Society, it was not in the end found possible to send out a Mission strong enough to undertake this new work, lying so far beyond. The disappointment at the time was very great, but there was no doubt in John's mind that the choice made was a wise one.

The more general question of the employment of African labourers in the mines, far
away from their homes, came up before
John in various forms during the latter
portion of his missionary career in Rhodesia,
especially after he had been stationed at
Bulawayo.

"Whenever," he writes, "the Europeans
start their mining operations, a very large
number of Africans, straight from the kraals,
flock to the work of the mines. They live
in the mining compounds under the most un-
natural conditions. For it is impossible to
transplant the old home life of the Africans
in its entirety into these new mining centres."

John goes on to explain the appalling conditions of the barracks, called " compounds,"
when he first took up this problem in Southern
Rhodesia, and determined not to let it go
on any further without a protest from the
Christian Church.

Tens of thousands of men, in the prime of
life, were brought to one mining centre from
hundreds of different kraals, in which hitherto
they had been leading a family life with their
wives and children. They were taken away
from this comparatively healthy normal life,
lived in the open air, where they had been engaged in agricultural pursuits, and set to

work under abnormal and unhealthy conditions underground, and made to reside in compounds which were the hotbeds of drunkenness, immorality and vice. Disease became rampant, spreading throughout the whole compound. When the men went back, they carried the disease germs away with them to the villages, infecting women and children. The terrible death-rates at the mines were thus reproduced in the kraals.

" Has the Christian Church," cries John with burning indignation at the tragedy of it all, " nothing to say to these evils ? Must we simply look on and hold our peace ? Can we do nothing to stop the flood of all this misery and sin ? Surely, just as we build churches and halls to meet the growing needs of the European population, which has problems of its own equally grave, so, in the same manner, we ought to provide religious and social ministrations for the tens of thousands of the African people who come from the kraals."

John then attacks the root of all the mischief—the greed of the European to get riches in order to keep up an artificial standard of comfort, and even luxury, in Europe.

" Our insatiable love of money," he cries, " which is a root of all evil, has brought them into this most undesirable condition. *We cannot stand by with folded arms and watch them going to moral ruin !* "

Such a course was unthinkable to a man like John White, in whose heart the love of Christ was burning at a white heat, and he set to work through the Missionary Conference, and its Standing Committee, and through every Christian agency which he could influence, to make known the terrible facts. He compared what was happening in Central Africa with the condition of things depicted by Mr. and Mrs. Hammond a century ago in England at the time of the Industrial Revolution. In those earlier days, in England itself, the human lives of women and children were counted so cheap that in a single generation the whole country-side of England was brought to the verge of moral ruin. Only when it was almost too late did the Christian conscience awake and stop the exploitation of the poor in this disgracefully unchristian manner.

In exactly the same way, John said, the African was being sacrificed, to-day before our very eyes, but because Africa was far away no one seemed to care anything about it. But God cared, and the mark of Cain, who murdered his brother, was on the brow of those who thought little of sacrificing their fellow men as long as they got their big dividends and their mining shares went up in the world market.

While, on tne one hand, John thus saw more clearly than anyone else at that time in Southern Rhodesia, the moral damage that was being done, and sought by every means in his power to prevent it, he did everything at the same time to make the most of each opportunity that was offered for the furtherance of the Gospel as the one final remedy for evils of this kind.

At first the mining authorities resisted every effort and were bitterly hostile to missionary work. But this stage rapidly passed away, because the mining companies themselves were soon faced with the moral damage done by their own compound system, which led on to grave physical evils. The threatened dearth in the supply of labour, if things went much further, made them pause; and the Government administrators, who were closely in touch with what was happening, refused to allow exploitation of this kind to go any farther. Furthermore, among the managers of these companies the moral conscience began to awake and reassert itself. For there were earnest Christian men among them.

So in the long run, the policy of the mines

became altered. The managers began to welcome the help of Missions and to give facilities for them, instead of preventing their evangelists and teachers from entering the compounds. We have just noticed an illustration of this, when the Belgian Governor —himself a Roman Catholic—was actually welcoming a Protestant Mission to take part in the settlement of a new mining township in the Congo in order to get all the humanitarian aid possible to help him in the new problems which faced him.

So John was able at last to send evangelists and teachers into the mining compounds themselves with the full consent of the companies concerned. These evangelists found a welcome response. Men from the mines, after their day's work was over, flocked to their meetings, and those who had heard about Christ in the mines carried back the good news to their own homes.

This was what Chikara had done, and the consequence, as we have seen, was the formation of a new mission station beyond the Zambesi.

" In the early days," John relates concerning another incident, " I was asked by some men to go and open a church close to the Tebekwe mine. The little building,

erected entirely by themselves, was packed
with people eager to hear the Gospel. Great
was their rejoicing. For I was the first
European missionary who had ever come to
see them and preach to them.

" About thirty miles away, there was
another place named Vungwe. The son of
the ruling chief had attended the opening
Gospel service of this new church at Tebekwe.
He became truly converted to God and was
called Peter when he was baptised. When
Peter went home he carried the glorious news
about Christ his Saviour with him.

" Soon, therefore, they had a new church
built at Vungwe. Peter, the son of the
chief, was sent eventually to be trained for
the ministry. He became one of the most
competent and reliable of our missionaries.
So the work goes on."

How arduous was the struggle, as John
pursued steadily his one great object, with
many apparent failures, and here and there a
great moral victory, can be traced in his own
letters and also in the records of the Missionary Conference. One example may be
given here. He writes : " Eighteen months
ago, a great deal of harm was being done at
the mines and other centres of employment
by a promiscuous clan, chiefly of Africans,

who had come from outside Rhodesia. They brewed and sold beer to the employees.

" The Government wanted to deal with this evil and drafted a Bill, which proposed to stop these Africans from selling, but would license the Europeans to do it.

" I brought to the notice of the Government and the public what I regarded as the inevitable evils of such a system ; how that the trade would draw the very lowest type of European, who would make it his business by adulteration and other means to enrich himself without any regard for the degradation of the African people. In a wide, wild country, like Rhodesia, anything like effective supervision would be impossible, and the latter state would be worse than the first.

" The Attorney General, who was very sympathetically disposed, sent for me and we discussed the matter fully. The result was a Bill (which finally became law) prohibiting the sale of all intoxicants to Africans outside the urban areas, but allowing employers, as they deemed it desirable, to issue the beer ration only to their own employees.

" This Act has changed completely many of the mine compounds from scenes—on Sunday especially—of bestiality and drunkenness to sober and respectable centres."

CHAPTER XVI : AT BULAWAYO

In the year 1913, John was obliged to return to England, in order to take a third furlough, and be again examined by the doctors. He was much weakened in health.

From this time onwards, we have repeated records of illnesses bravely borne. Only his wife knew how much each extra strain told upon him. Nothing but a supreme devotion to his Lord and Master, whom he served night and day, kept him steadfast to his work in the mission field, while the burden, within and without, went on increasing. He kept up a courageous heart and showed only cheerful good humour to the outside world; but those who knew him best, understood what weariness he had to endure on account of his failing health.

When he went home, in 1913, no one in London was able to detect what was the underlying cause of his illness. But it would now appear that the malignant growth, which proved fatal in the end, had all along been very deep-seated, and that its presence could only be discovered later.

Before the tragedy of the World War began,
in August, 1914, John and his wife had returned to Rhodesia. This time, partly for
health and other reasons, he was stationed
in Bulawayo. Life there, it was hoped,
could be lived under somewhat less exacting
conditions.

But his illness came back once more, in
1916, and this caused him to undertake,
much against his will, another journey to
England for special treatment. It was a
sad time for him and for all, because the War
was at its height, but after a short period at
home, he was allowed to return to Africa, and
there he remained at Bulawayo doing some
of his most devoted and unselfish work and
coming into touch with many Europeans
who became his friends.

Hitherto, John's active work in the mission
field had been farther north, among the
Mashona people, who had learnt to love and
trust him. But now, at Bulawayo, he was
in the heart of the Matabele country and was
called upon to exercise his ministry, not among
the village people, away from the towns, but
in a rapidly rising township, with large railway works, mines and factories on every side.

New problems stared him in the face. He
was close to the Matoppo Hills, where

Rhodes and Jameson lay buried. Bulawayo was the exact spot, which Rhodes had chosen from the very first, to be his chief mining and railway centre of the new territory.

Was all this rapid development, which Rhodes had fostered, good or bad? What did it all mean in the eyes of God, Who is no respecter of persons? Was it the will of God that one race should dominate over another in this manner, forcing the weaker race into an inferior and almost servile position? Was it right for the stronger to impose his will on the weaker? Was that the law of Christ?

In Mashonaland the one main issue at stake had been the preservation of the land for the Mashona tribes. But here, as we have seen in the last chapter, the problem went far deeper and was more fundamental. The African was uprooted. How could he take root again?

John was able to study in Bulawayo, at first hard, what the impact of the European industrial civilisation, in its most aggressive form, had meant to the original inhabitants of the country. He found the African, who had been dispossessed by the European, cut off from all his old tribal habits and caught up in the meshes of a modern economic system, from which there seemed to be absolutely no escape. Without any strong religious background to hold him fast his moral life crumbled to pieces. The worst animal passions were excited, and little that was good remained.

Even those who had been converted to Christ and were leading Christian lives, found it hard to resist the disintegration caused by an entirely new form of existence. Life, for the African, was being forced into an entirely new and uncommon groove at an alarming speed and there was no one to stand by his side and help him, as an elder brother, to solve his own problems.

In this vital respect, John found that the Christian faith itself had lost much of its ancient power to heal, because of the racial barrier which separated European from African Christians. " We, then, that are strong," St. Paul had said to the Christians at Rome, " ought to bear the infirmities of the weak and not to please ourselves."[1] But here, in Rhodesia, a cleavage had taken place within the Church itself, which destroyed the unity of the Body of Christ. Instead of the stronger European helping the weaker African, who had only just begun to learn of Christ and

[1] Rom. xv. 1.

to call Him Master, such a gulf had widened between them, that hardly any mutual Christian contact and intercourse remained.

Indeed, the racial division had become so accentuated into what were sometimes called " white " and " black " churches, that the religion practised even by professing Christians fell far short of the Gospel of Christ. It would have hardly been recognised as Christian in the apostolic days.

For the Apostle Paul had laid it down in quite unmistakable terms, that " As many as have been baptised into Christ have put on Christ. There can be neither Jew nor Greek . . . for ye are all one Man in Christ Jesus."[1] And again the same Apostle declares, " Ye have put on the new Man . . . where there is neither Greek nor Jew, Barbarian, Scythian, bond nor free, but Christ is all and in all."[2]

So strongly did St. Paul feel this that he vehemently proclaimed on this very subject : " If any man preach unto you any other gospel, let him be anathema. . . . The Gospel, which I preached unto you, is not of man, but by revelation of Jesus Christ."[3] And when Peter came down to Antioch and refused to eat with the Gentiles, Paul " with-

[1] Gal. iii. 28.   [2] Col. iii. 10, 11.   [3] Gal. i. 9–12.

stood him to his face, because he was to be blamed."[1]

All this John had known by heart from the lectures on St. Paul in Didsbury College, which he had listened to with eager attention long ago. When he found out that there had been a weakening, in face of the racial and colour prejudice, among Christians themselves, it overwhelmed him with unutterable shame, as bringing dishonour to the name of Christ. Therefore he set his face against it like a flint.

It was my great privilege, while in Southern Rhodesia, in 1934, to stay with those in Bulawayo who had been brought under John White's personal influence in these and other matters, and to hear from them what a tower of strength he had been. Everywhere the story of his modesty and lowliness of heart, combined with his invincible courage and almost reckless daring, was told me. Above all, I was told that he was adamant when any question of "race" or "colour" was concerned. He was ready to die, if need be, as a martyr on that one issue!

Little children loved him and called him "Uncle John." His affection for them in return was one of the deepest things in his

[1] Gal. ii. 11.

nature. Indeed, wherever he went, he was richly blest in winning almost at sight the hearts of children of every race, who seemed to find out instinctively the warmth of the love in his own heart towards them. They brought Christ very near to him because Christ Himself was the lover of little children.

Towards his fellow Christians who were Africans by race, he was so utterly free from any pride or self-esteem, or superiority as a European, that they trusted him just as little children did ; for they were themselves childlike by nature. He always treated them with a natural courtesy and dignity and equality that made Christ's own love understood among them. Thus in his own character, as seen in his daily life, he revealed in a living way " the meekness and gentleness of Christ " to those who were still weak in the faith and needed every encouragement.

One of the younger missionaries, who worked with great devotion under John White, was the Rev. G. H. B. Sketchley. He tells us that John captured the hearts of all those men and women, when they came out for the first time to the mission field, by his complete humility and personal modesty, while exceeding all others in the sacrifices he made for the mission cause. These are the traits in his character—along with his sense of humour—which are repeated in all the accounts that have been written about him.

The picture that G. H. B. Sketchley draws adds another feature which is equally true. He represents him as one who was at all times desperately intent on making peace between the races, while taking his place, on every occasion, by the side of the weaker race. He refused to compromise, in the slightest degree, where he felt the Christian faith itself was at stake. Once and for all, the mighty struggle for Christian liberty for the African, within the one Body of Christ, had to be fought and won. The " middle wall of partition "[1] had to be broken down.

Just as the Apostle Paul himself had fought that great " good fight of faith," which had resulted in the Gentile Christians being regarded as " no more strangers and aliens, but fellow citizens with the saints and of the household of God,"[2] so now John strove to the same end on behalf of his beloved African converts. Just as the struggle to overcome the sharp division, which Judaism had made in the Early Church, was no secondary issue, but a matter of life and death, even so it was now in Africa.

[1] Eph. ii. 14.   [2] Eph. ii. 19.

" I first met John White," writes G. H. B. Sketchley, " when I arrived in Bulawayo fresh from England. That was the beginning of a friendship which remained unbroken all through. One of the first incidents I can recall was the arrival in Bulawayo of a large number of Baralong girls from Maroka's Stadt, near Francistown. These girls, who had been trained in housework, were in great demand for domestic service in European houses, and John's telephone was kept busy answering calls.

" But before he would consent to put one of these girls out in service, he always ascertained whether accommodation was available under her employer's own roof. Unless that was assured he would not recommend.

" Later on, being ably supported by Mrs. White, a hostel was built for these girls near our church. It is to be regretted that the Hostel did not meet with the support from the girls themselves which it deserved; but that was no fault of John White's.

" He rarely preached in the European Church, and never did so if his younger colleague was in town and available. I have never ceased to wonder at the humility wherewith he would read over his sermons to me and ask to be corrected. That humility

was characteristic of·the man and sometimes
led people to mistake his great capacities.

" When I arrived in Southern Rhodesia, he
told me what my work would be and then
said to me in characteristic fashion :

" ' That's *your* job. I shan't interfere.
If ever you get into difficulties come to me,
and I will do my best for you.'

" Thus we had two years of the happiest
companionship in Bulawayo. He had a
delightful gift of humour, and no man more
appreciated a good joke, even though it was
told against himself. I rarely came away
without being richer for one really good
story, as well as abundantly richer in the
deeper things of life. For one could not be
near John White for long without realising
that he was ' far ben.'

" It is a joy to recall several rides with him
through rough country. Although he suffered
from digestive trouble, he had a sturdy frame
and could stand a great amount of fatigue.
In the days before motor-cars came into use,
he would stay on the trail as long as any of us
younger men.

" It was a delight to have him in the
home with us. He had a wonderful love for
children, and in my own family was always
known as ' Uncle John.'

" We had the great privilege of entertaining him and his wife for the last days of his long stay in Southern Rhodesia. From early morning to late at night, the house was besieged by callers, African and European alike, who came to wish him farewell. Few of us will ever forget the amazing vigour with which he preached to us on his last Sunday evening in Bulawayo. It was hard to believe that he was then suffering from a fatal disease.

" His visit to the African Church in the afternoon was in the nature of a royal triumph, and we had almost to drag him away from the people who crowded round him, lest he should become overtired.

" There is one English phrase that has a peculiar significance in Rhodesia. It is carved on the last resting-place of those who are called 'great,' in the Matoppo Hills. The words are, ' Who have deserved well of their country.' Sir Fraser Russell, the Chief Justice, applied that phrase to John White, who richly merited it.

" For twenty-five years he carried the burden of Chairmanship of the District, as well as the work of Superintendent. During part of the time he added to these the Principalship of Waddilove Institution. Few men have ever worked harder or more unselfishly.

" He commanded always the respect even of those who differed from him most strongly. When his work came to its close he had a host of friends, not only among those for whom he chiefly laboured, but among the European population also."

One of the dearest of these European friends who came often to see John during his last illness was Archibald Underwood. The affection between them was very touching to witness. On one occasion Archie Underwood brought his son so that he might receive help and blessing from such a visit.

As soon as ever these two old friends got together, John seemed at once to revive. He would be full of anecdotes, and one story would follow another in quick succession. Afterwards he would suffer for it in some measure, because it tried him more than he could bear ; but in other ways it cheered him and did him good.

It was a great privilege to me to be present when friends such as Archie Underwood came to visit John, and I have a very vivid memory of these meetings. For one delightful trait in John's character stood out prominently on such occasions, namely, his large-hearted human kindness. In all his flow of anecdote he was brimming over with

fun and good humour, without a single word
that could hurt anyone's feelings. He would
speak in a generous manner even of those
who had bitterly opposed him. For John
could keep no bitterness in his own heart ;
it was not in his nature to do so.

Many who enter the ministry of the Church
when they are young—as John did—seem to
lose after a time their natural manner and
human touch. Their very speech and accent
tend to become " clerical." John was far
too simple and direct for any such change to
happen to him. He remained always a man
among men, enjoying life to the full, so long
as his health enabled him to do so, and even
in times of illness keeping his brave spirit full
of brightness to the last.

Yet this did not make him any the less
deeply reverent and devout whenever, in the
varied daily round, the appointed hour of
worship came. He could pass easily from
grave to gay, and gay to grave. He knew
how to relax after a period of straining high
in thought and word either in the church or
in private devotion, and this was a precious
gift. His naturally devout nature was, in this
way, never overwrought. The true balance
was kept. He could alter his whole attitude
in a moment from merry laughter to the

most solemn subjects with the simplicity one
sees in little children. This was no effort to
him, because his thoughts of his Heavenly
Father were essentially childlike and ever
near at hand. He could laugh with joy in
God's presence as well as stand in awe of
Him and fear Him.

All this I had noticed for myself, but it
came out still more clearly when he was in
the company of old friends whom he loved.
At Bulawayo, when I visited those who knew
him and asked about his ministry, it was
always this human side that was brought
most prominently before me. Everyone
recognised that he was a man of God, instant
in prayer, fervent in spirit, serving the
Lord; but this lovable human side had
impressed people most of all. As I have
related, he was " Uncle John " to all who
were with him, and not to children alone.

After the Sunday which I had spent in
Bulawayo was over, and I had spoken from
the pulpit where he used to preach, his
friends met me and we remained up to a
very late hour talking about him. All that
he had done in Rhodesia was still fresh in
men's minds, and I heard about the bitter
opposition he had been obliged to encounter
on behalf of the Africans in Bulawayo itself.

His love for them was profound and they trusted him as their Father.

Other stories were told me about his devotion to duty and utter self-sacrifice at the time of the great influenza epidemic which came at the end of the War. Though himself in very feeble health at that time, he had never spared himself for a moment, ministering to African and European alike until he caught the infection. The severe and unremitting strain of those days told heavily upon him. He never quite recovered from them in the later years.

In 1919 he was obliged to leave the work at Bulawayo and go back to Waddilove Institute, but his sickness still possessed him, and he could not do the immense amount of work which he had been used to do in earlier days.

Thus, in 1921, he said farewell to Africa in such a state of physical prostration that few expected to see him return. On this critical journey home it was only the unceasing care of Mrs. White which enabled him to reach England at all. Before his marriage, he had never taken any trouble about his health or looked after himself, and now he owed it to the devotion of his wife that his life was preserved.

CHAPTER XVII **¡** THE FAMINE

WHILE John White had already gained the affection of the Mashona people as no European had done by many well-remembered deeds of bravery and human kindness, it was the famine in 1922 that cemented their devotion to him and made him known throughout Rhodesia as a man of God.

The story of the famine is told by one of the Christian converts, G. Siqalaba, an evangelist of the Marandellas District.

" The great incident," he writes, " which made me realise that Baba White had given his life for the African people was this :

" It was in the year 1922 that the people in the Reserves suffered from starvation. Right through the whole of Rhodesia, people were dying. Many men ran to the Native Commissioner. Except in Marandellas District, there were not many who got their help from the Native Commissioner, because of this simple reason : People who first met him and asked for help were told to work on the roads first, which go through the Reserve.

" On that account many people left his help and went to Baba White for assistance.

" When Baba White heard so many people who wanted to be helped, crying for food, he ordered nearly three hundred bags of mealie meal from Salisbury. Each bag of meal cost him about fifteen shillings, or even more than that.

" Some people, when they heard this, came to Waddilove even before the bags had arrived. They would wait at Baba White's door for two or three days. While they were still waiting Baba White would give them some mealie meal for themselves. When the bags had come at last, he would send a message round throughout the Reserve. At the time, when the people had gathered together, he gave to each of them according to the number of bags that he required.

" Women who had no husbands—he would give to them first. He did not wait for something from them, but gave them the mealie meal as a free gift. Even to those who were able to return him something, Baba White did not ask first how much money each man had got. He gave to everyone of them the bags without taking money first. Then afterwards he said to them, ' When your good time comes, I would like to see each of you show his gratitude in some way or other.'

" When I look back on that time, I can see how all the people thought of thanking Baba White because of what he did for them in the famine. People did not even cover the expense he bore when buying the bags. But the idea of Baba White was not for the gaining of money. It was based on saving the people from starvation."

The same famine of 1922 is referred to by Andria Shamu, who had been with John White a long time and knew him well.

" Baba White," he writes in a letter, " hated lies with every drop of his blood. Theft and jealousy he hated also, and many of his sermons and addresses were made up about these.

" He believed in prayer—prayer in secret to God, and also public prayer. He went out every morning to talk to God in secret in the bush.

" His name is inwardly written on our foreheads. He loved us, both young and old. He was straightforward in all his dealings. He showed me the love of Jesus. His actions interpreted every word he spoke, and so I was able to understand the love of Jesus from his actions.

" He used to travel from village to village by ox-wagon, and speak to us around out fire-places. At first we laughed at him, but afterwards we learnt to pray ourselves.

" In 1922 there was a famine throughout the whole of Southern Rhodesia, so that many were dying. Baba White purchased grain from the Government, at Salisbury, with his own money and fed the people of the Marandellas District. Though all promised to pay him back, when the time of plenty came, only a few refunded him for his outlay. But he did not mind this. The Mashona people are very grateful to Baba White for this service of love.

" Sometimes his ox-wagon used to break down, and Baba White would send back messengers for food. Often he went without food, waiting beside his wagon. Before he was married, he used to eat the same food that the Mashona people eat.

" He fed us at the time of starvation.

" He healed my eldest son whom he took for a month under his special care. Our hearts are full of thanks as we look at Waddilove, which is the ' child ' of Baba White, and we are thankful also that his remains lie buried in the churchyard at Waddilove.

" We feel his presence with us every day, and wherever he is with God he still notices all we do to bring forward the Kingdom of God in our land."

While I was at Waddilove I heard the story of that famine year, how, with a noble recklessness, trusting in God alone, John had gone far beyond his resources in providing corn to save the people he loved from starvation. It is true that he did not receive much in return of actual money, in comparison with what he spent, but he was able to preserve from death a great number of the Mashona people in their kraals, and the gratitude which he received more than amply repaid him for the money payments which he was unable afterwards to recover.

The years that followed the famine year were among the most fruitful in John's whole ministry as a missionary among the people. He was able to see, with a grateful heart, how God had prospered all his handiwork. With the Psalmist he could say :

" Not unto us, O Lord, not unto us, but unto Thy Name give the praise, for Thy loving-mercy and for Thy truth's sake."

The elder brother of Andria Shamu was blind and lived in " Border Church " village[1] near to Waddilove. A very deep affection sprang up between John White and Jack Shamu, Andria's brother. John had arranged for several Christian families, including

[1] See chapter ix, 104.

Jack Shamu's family, to reside on the Mission Farm, which was not far away from his own house. He allowed them to draw their drinking water from his own tank. Thus Jack would come constantly into touch with his friend John White, and they prayed and had fellowship together.

Jack relates how John White used to open up new villages to the Gospel message in a very simple manner. He used to go about with an ox-wagon loaded with bags of salt, cheap blankets, slates and books. By making little presents he would attract the people to him. When they asked what things he had to sell, supposing him to be a trader, he would tell them that he had come to bring to them the love of Jesus which was freely offered to them, without money and without price.

Jack Shamu relates further, how John White would take special care of all who were sick. So much did they value his service, and so closely did they watch his life, as he went about doing good in Christ's name, that the people of the villages called him " Man of God." If anyone was sick, as soon as ever John White heard about it, he visited the village and did his best to heal the sick person.

" The biggest thing of all," said Jack
Shamu, " was this : that John White taught
us to pray and to know Jesus.[1]   I first learnt
about Jesus from John White."

Even when the work of Waddilove and
other administrative duties pressed hard upon
him, John never left for any length of time
his village people.   He would train his evangelists at Waddilove by taking two or three
of them round with him on tour, utilising
their services in new translation work and
also sitting down with them among the
villagers, when the day's journey was over,
in order to speak about the wonderful love
of Jesus.   No word of life had ever come to
them like this before.

Out of the midst of scenes like these John
went to Salisbury, in 1926, to preside as Chairman at the Missionary Conference.   Here he
made one of the finest of all his addresses.

" Like the first apostles," he said, " we are
to preach Jesus and the Resurrection.   On
that point there is no divergence of opinion
among us.   We may utter our message with
varying emphasis, but the ultimate truth is
one—we offer salvation in Christ to sinful,
dying men.   This, it seems to me, was the
complete task of the African missionary of

[1] See chapter xix, p. 231.

fifty to a hundred years ago. To an un-awakened race, he was the herald of good news : he spoke of personal deliverance from degrading superstition and every evil habit. Compared with our work now, his was a very simple one.

"But will anyone urge, in this era of Africa's awakening, that this represents our entire obligation and responsibility ? Have we nothing to say to our people about the right solution of these unaccustomed problems with which they are suddenly confronted ?

"We have preached to them Jesus. Have we nothing to tell them about the *spirit* in which Jesus Christ would meet these diffi-culties ? I think St. Paul would have con-sidered any other interpretation of His ministry much too restricted. . . .

"We have spoken of the Africans, as a race, awakening to a consciousness of their dignity as men, yea, as sons of God. But they, on their side, must understand that if they have emerged from the dark and become children of the light, they must walk in the light. They must put away the things that bring them into bondage-sloth, drunkenness, polygamy, forced marriage and witchcraft. ' For freedom hath Christ made us free '—

this must be our message for the awakening
Bantu race.

" Equally, on the other side, there is a
Christian message for the governing European
race. From Scripture it is clear that God
does not give us any infallible, stereotyped
plan for the settlement of the problems that
may arise. He does, however, lay down for
us great principles of justice and righteousness for our guidance. No settlement of
racial and other problems can ignore these
principles. On them the foundations must
rest. It is the duty of the Christian leader
to make this quite clear. He must sound an
alarm. Like the prophets of olden days, he
must preach righteousness to the nation, as
well as to the individual. As God gives us
light, we are to apply the teaching of our
Lord Jesus Christ to the needs of the present
hour. Africa's awakening has created a situation which He alone can solve in a manner
that will ensure peace and satisfaction to all
concerned. In the inscrutable mystery of
Divine Providence this task has become
peculiarly ours. We dare not set it aside."

With a definite purpose I have set down
in this chapter, side by side, first of all, the
simple witness of different African Christians,
one after another, telling in their own way

what specially endeared John to them as a man of God, thus winning their heart's affection. Then afterwards I have given his own noble utterance at Salisbury, where those in authority, engaged in thinking out the deepest problems in race relations, were present. In either case, John brings back the whole issue to the life and teaching our Lord and Saviour, Jesus Christ.

Whether he is passing through the Mashona villages, healing the sick and ministering to the famine-striken multitude, or boldly preaching before those in authority in high places concerning " righteousness, temperance and judgment to come,"[1] his eyes are fixed upon that one Figure of the Son of Man, who came to seek and save that which was lost.

" For," as St. Paul himself told us, " the divine Yes has at last sounded in Him. For in Him is the Yes that affirms all the promises of God. Hence it is through Him that we affirm our Amen in worship to the glory of God."[2]

---

[1] Acts xxiv. 25.   [2] 2 Cor. i. 20 (Moffat).

CHAPTER XVIII : THE FRIEND OF THE FRIENDLESS

No one could doubt for a moment John White's entire devotion to his Lord and Saviour Jesus Christ, to whom he had dedicated his life. No one, again, could question that he was absorbed heart and soul in his life-work of spreading the Gospel among the villages of Mashonaland and in the regions beyond.

With the Apostle Paul he could truly say : "Necessity is laid upon me ; yea, woe is me if I preach not the Gospel." [1] The love of Christ constrained him so completely that he was under what was to him a divine compulsion to do this work of God in Africa.

Yet he gave himself with equally direct earnestness to the wider field, wherein he sought with every power he possessed to save the Africans, whom he loved, from being oppressed or defrauded by those who ruled over them ; and in this latter work some, whom he deeply respected, had scruples as to

[1] 1 Cor. ix. 16.

whether he was doing the genuine missionary service for which he had been ordained.

John felt this criticism very keenly and wrote several papers and letters about it, from which I have been able to take much of what follows in this chapter.

" It has been urged," he states, " that the missionary induces criticism and sometimes censure by ' meddling in political matters outside his province.' He has been sent, it is contended, to preach the Gospel and minister to the people in spiritual things, and thus any activity outside this prescribed circle should be to him strictly taboo. He should content himself with declaring a message of personal salvation ; but the application of the Gospel of our Lord and Saviour Jesus Christ to the corporate and national life of the people, to whom he came to preach, should be left to those who have made politics their special business."

John gladly recognised that there was much to be said for a minister of religion leaving politics on one side in a country like England or Scotland, where everyone has an elementary education and receives a vote, and has been taught, at least in some measure, to think and act for himself. A true and earnest minister of the Gospel, in that case, would find his primary duty so exacting that he would have little time for anything else.

Also, where party politics were concerned, there was much that went on with which no minister of religion would care to be too closely associated. For the man of God had always to avoid the lower level of compromise, which politics often implied, and to set up instead the uncompromising higher principle and then let it work.

With all this John would entirely agree. But in modern Africa, as it was rapidly being opened up by European exploitation, the missionary, whose first duty was towards the African people themselves, was in an entirely different position from that of a parish minister at home who had charge of a settled congregation.

He had to be, in every sense of the word, the true *friend* of the African, who had no other friend so near to him in his hour of greatest distress and danger. For to-day the African was voiceless, voteless and defenceless, and the soil which was all he had in the world was at stake.

The European, on the other hand, who had taken possession of the greater part of the soil, had all the power in his own hands. He could do what he liked, and he was almost

entirely ignorant of the harm he was doing,
because he had no close understanding of
the African whom he was dispossessing. If
the missionary, who knew the African at
close quarters and could speak his language,
did not stand up for him, then who else
would do so ?

Still further than this, these very Europeans
who were dispossessing the Africans went each
Sunday to the Christian Church and called
themselves Christians, in the midst of an
African population which was still predomi-
nantly " heathen " in the true sense of the
term.   Whatever acts the European did were
naturally regarded by this African world as
a part of their Christian profession.   Yet
acts which might clearly lead to un-Christian
injustice towards the Africans were being
perpetrated daily because the rulers of the
country, who professed and called themselves
Christians, had not realised their full Christian
responsibilities.

Therefore John White, who had learnt to
understand " where the shoe pinched " among
his African converts, was determined to think
out this whole matter afresh and not to be
satisfied with analysis taken from mission
work at home in a country like England or
Scotland.   The new conditions in Africa

demanded a new application of Christ's eternal Gospel.

Someone, whose impartiality was beyond question, had to take up the African cause in all its aspects, so as not to allow it to go by default. No one, in the emergency which had arisen was in a better position than the missionary to do this. For he understood intimately the language and the customs of the people. He lived near them and was not feared, but rather trusted by them ; and trust begets confidence, while fear destroys it. The Lord Jesus Christ Himself "went about doing good and healing all manner of diseases." He was always the " friend of the friendless." He would to-day be standing on the side of the African at this time when the African was suffering, through ignorance and misunderstanding, and He would say to the Europeans, " Inasmuch as ye did it unto the least of these, My brethren, ye did it unto Me."

John thought all this out afresh as he, too, stood, in his Master's name, on the side of the African. The more he thought it over, the more he felt the need, in his Master's name, of becoming in every sense of the word, " the friend of the friendless." To take up their cause, therefore, along with his intimate

companion, Arthur Cripps, was not " meddling
in politics " as the words are used in England.
It was taking rather up the Cross of misunderstanding and rejection, which his Lord
and Saviour carried. It meant, once for all,
the laying down of the great foundation principles of Christian justice between the races,
without which the whole structure of human
society in Rhodesia would fall to the ground.

" If," said John White truly, " we are to
be the real helpers of these backward people,
I cannot see how we can possibly divest ourselves of our responsibility. Like our Master,
Jesus Christ, we must be ' the friendless
people's friend.' But let us make no mistake
about the burden we take on our own
shoulders. Every quality of heart and mind
that we possess must be consecrated to this
great task.

" How little does the most experienced of
us know about the ambitions, the aspirations,
the ideals of our African constituency ! Yet
it we are really to help them, however difficult
the task, we must apply ourselves earnestly
to it. Not only so but in a country like
Rhodesia we must be prepared to look at
all these problems through the eyes of the
European settler also. We must hold the
balance even."

John then went on to describe the difficulties which this involved and the dangers in the missionary's path. Some missionaries brought a stain on the name of Christ by their weak acquiescence and dependence on Europeans who had all the power in their hands and were actively using it for the subjection of the Africans, dispossessing them from the soil, which was their very life blood. Thus they seemed to the Africans themselves to be taking sides against them.

The actions, John stated, of all missionaries ought to be free from suspicions of this kind. Their motives, from the African side, ought to be entirely above reproach. Whatever was done, should be done for the good of the African and for the glory of God.

In all that John wrote at this time he kept on continually affirming with all his might that the whole future of the masses of the African people, as well as their moral welfare, was bound up with the fair division and partition of the land between the African and the European. If things went wrong in that direction, they would be likely to go wrong all round.

For the African was a great lover of the soil. He clung to it, as John saw, with the heart's affection of a peasant people. John himself could sympathise with them in his own heart, for he, too, loved the soil of his own Cumberland dales with his own heart's affection, and therefore was so near to the Mashona in all that he said and did on their behalf.

If the African became landless he would either sink down to a serf-like condition on some European's farm, or else he would drift into the mines or the towns and become rapidly in danger of losing his moral character, and along with it some of his best qualities as the member of a great race.

The missionaries' duty, therefore, at this most critical time of all was to help these people, over whom they had pastoral care, to secure an adequate amount of good agricultural land, not only for their own families and tribes, but also for their descendants.

John believed that no more tragic blunder had been made throughout South Africa than the neglect of this primary duty towards their own people in earlier days by the missionaries who were the natural protectors of the Bantu race. Thousands of dispossessed and detribalised people had become landless serfs without ever having a hope in the future of a settled home of their own. How could *these* build up a church ?

This tragedy of Africa farther south must not be allowed to happen again in Rhodesia. The danger was imminent. It was already happening in Kenya. Where was it to stop?

If it was argued that w 'k of this kind was not the missionary's fu. .ion, then John answered bluntly: " If a house is on fire does a missionary merely stand by and preach? Does he not take the lead in putting out the fire? In the great emergency in Rhodesia, whose function is it to protect the rights of the Mashona? "

As a Cumberland farmer, John could make this declaration about the land with a strong conviction. And in the long run he was able to carry conviction to others.

From this grave question of a landless proletariat drifting helplessly from one occupation to another, John turn to the still more vital question of justice.

" Must the African always be dumb? " he asks. " Must he allow his case constantly to go by default? We may not be prepared to broaden the basis of the franchise, but there must be *some* method devised whereby his needs and grievances can be uttered. This, too, is his heritage.

" Justice in our Law Courts and fair treatment in the administration of the law are surely legal rights in any British colony. Here again the utmost vigilance is necessary.

" In matters of judicial administration there has been from the beginning a great necessity for the missionary to watch the interests of the African. There have been cases before the Law Courts where it was clear, on evidence, that a European had committed murder; but the jury (a European one) failed to find guilty. Many cases of this kind could be quoted; and, but for the fact that the missionaries were constantly on their guard and made some kind of protest, these cases might have been multiplied.

" There was a case, for instance, in which a native was found trespassing on a white man's property. He was arrested by the owner, fastened to a tree and flogged. He died from his injuries. The European was tried and let off with a short period of imprisonment.

" One other occasion is the instance of a European killing a native; though the accused pleaded guilty, the jury brought in a verdict of not guilty. So surprised was the judge that on giving his decision he turned to the jury and said : " Gentlemen, I would advise you to go home and read carefully the Ten Commandments."

When the jury system led to such atrocious injustice as that, it was obviously impossible to continue to use it where a racial issue was involved, for the dice were loaded against the African, and so this system of trial was stopped. But this had not succeeded in bringing about justice. John asserted (and no one knew the facts better than he did) that sometimes methods of a third degree kind were used upon witnesses in order to make them witness for the prosecution when they had really appeared to give evidence for the accused.

Even if the gross injustice of early police methods of this kind had died down, yet all was not yet as it should be. A sense of injustice was rankling in the Africans' hearts because of the treatment which they often received and the heavy penalties imposed.

John brings forward a peculiarly odious case where an African house servant, who had been bidden by his mistress to take a message to her friend as quickly as he could, rode his bicycle through Abercorn Street, in Bulawayo, a little faster than the law thought he should do, and was fined £5, which was, roughly, three months' wages. " Is it likely," asks John, " that a European for a similar default would be made to pay £75 fine which would be the proportionate amount ? "

The whole statement from which I have quoted shows how John's great strength lay in his superb sense of fair play, and how thoroughly he understood the details of every question that affected the Mashona people. In conclusion he mentions two larger issues where the pronounced opposition on the part of Arthur Cripps and himself, supported by other missionaries, had either prevented unfair legislation, or nullified it through arousing widespread disapproval.

In the first instance, the Government had drafted a Bill for the compulsory registration of African preachers who wished to preach in Rhodesia. The main idea of the Government was to prevent all sorts of curious religious sects coming into the country from South Africa. But in effect the Bill made the Native Affairs Department the judge of a good or bad " Gospel."

" Shearly Cripps and I," John writes, " felt strongly that this form of slavery to the Government regulation could not be tolerated. Such an enactment would mean that an African Christian, feeling inwardly moved to proclaim his own religious experience to his own people, would be prevented from so doing until he had got a Government permit. Our opposition to the measure was so persistent that the Government withdrew it.

" The second case was that in which the Government sought to indenture African male children to Europeans, and the penalty to be imposed upon these piccaninnies for any disobedience or wilfulness was whipping. This was to bring in a criminal punishment for a civil offence. Opposition was raised by the Missionary Conference, though even there all missionaries were not unanimous on the point. Pressure was brought to bear on the Government by considerable publicity in England exposing the puerility of this measure. As a result, though the Act was passed, the opposition raised made it difficult for the Government to carry it out, and the Act has fallen into disuse."

In an autobiographical passage of great value, John goes over the same subject again from a different angle. It will be seen from this passage also how the land question in Mashonaland is all important.

" When a youth," John writes, " on my father's farm, and afterwards, when in a theological college, my political sympathies were with the Left Wing of the Radical

Party. I felt that this Party supremely cared for the poorer people. They were the helpers of the 'under dog,' and for that reason what political sympathy I had was thrown in with them when I entered South Africa. Here I discovered that the bottom dog was the black man. He was obviously suffering from grave disabilities. His rights in the land were overlooked; the Law Courts gave him little justice; socially he was ostracised; and the general administration of native affairs was in a very unsatisfactory condition.

"I made this further discovery—that the African had no means of ventilating his wrongs. In England, the poor and the unjustly treated have a vote, and there is a chance for them to make known their grievances through those who represent them; but the African people cannot speak for themselves, nor have they anyone to stand up in their defence. Their position is a very difficult one. Racial feeling is so strong and bitter that in many cases the ordinary man jeopardises his business, social standing and other things that he values if he takes the side of the African.

"One of the first questions that came to my notice was that of the African's right to his own land—or, at least, to some of it. A system of semi-segregation had been instituted, and 7,000,000 acres of land had been set aside for the Africans. A slight glance at the facts revealed how utterly inadequate such a small portion was to meet their needs.

" There being nearly 1,000,000 Africans in the country, such an apportionment of land would imply at first sight that each of them could occupy seven acres of land, which certainly seems a fair amount. But the facts of the case are that, generally speaking, these Native Reserves have been mapped out in the most hilly and least fertile parts of the country—land which is obviously of little value to European farmers but quite good enough for the African. It can be seen, therefore, that the amount of really useful land is reduced to a very small area.

" We advocated an extension of the Native Reserves. This question the Government would not face, but considered the possibility of setting aside 1,000,000 acres of land in various places, portions of which land could be purchased as farms by the more enterprising Africans. The conditions of such land apportionment were that they were to be precluded from buying land in an area where Europeans were established. This to my mind was not at all satisfactory or adequate.

" Arthur Shearly Cripps was the champion in this fight. He was the leader in demanding that a better provision should be made. I was very glad to stand at his side and do what I could. But the fact still remains that the native of the country has not got a fair share of the land to which he is entitled."

There was one single rule that John White applied on every occasion and by which he was always guided. He would never, without a protest, allow any law to be brought forward, either in Church or State, which made any discrimination on the grounds of colour alone. Any " colour " legislation found him up in arms at once, as the champion of those who were being discriminated against.

" Not only," he says, " are we to preach to our own people deliverance from personal sin, but we must show them that Christ's Life and teaching have to do with the *whole* of life's affairs. If the great principles which Christ laid down are being contravened by those in authority, we must firmly and faithfully tell them so. On the other hand, if our African people find that they are the victims of oppression, we must courageously defend them or else we are unworthy of the Name we bear."

In carrying out these principles, few missionaries were prepared to go to the lengths that John White adopted. But everyone knew beforehand what he would say when a question of race or colour was involved. For he was adamant on this issue, and in a country where nearly every question is decided by Europeans on a colour or racial basis, it made his own attitude seem one of perpetual conflict.

If John were asked, as he often was, " By what authority do you make this principle so absolute ? " he would answer that it was essentially implied in Christ's own character as the Son of Man. Christ was all in all. In Him, the apostle wrote, " there can be neither Greek nor Jew, Barbarian, Scythian, bond nor free, but Christ is all and in all."

This was, to John, the charter of Christian liberty, the freedom wherewith Christ has made us free. " Suppose," he said, " we had been born ' coloured,' and suppose we were treated in the same way that the Europeans treat the coloured races, how should we like it ? "

If (he goes on) it is perfectly clear to us

that we would *not* like it, then let us apply at
once the Golden Rule of Christ and do to
others as we should wish them to do to us.
If we put ourselves in the other man's place,
at once the law of Christian love applies.
Therefore we must cease to be racial.

Or again, he would turn to the text, " For
one is your Master, even Christ : and all ye
are brethren." It was impossible, he said,
to call Christ " Lord, Lord," and then constantly to offend the least of His brethren.
Christ stood by the side of the African and
said to the European, " Inasmuch as ye have
done this unto the least of these My brethren,
ye have done it unto Me." It was, therefore,
not the African only that we were injuring by
our racial pride, but Christ Himself.

One of the noblest gifts which came to
John from his Christian faith was his power
of seeing Christ, his Lord and Master, before
him in the downtrodden races of the world.
To him they were not to be despised as
savages, even in their degradation, as they
lived without His grace ; but they were men
and women to be loved and redeemed, to be
sanctified and cleansed from sin.

Like St. Francis of Assisi, John saw Christ
Himself in the poor and naked, the sick and
the stranger, the outcast and the despised,

the tormented and oppressed.   Christ pleaded
with him, out of their very eyes, saying :

Is it nothing to you, all ye that pass by ?
Behold and see if there is any sorrow,
Like unto My sorrow.

And when he saw thus, with the mind of
Christ, then the love of the Crucified constrained him.   Instead of shrinking back from
their sorrow, or leaving them and passing
them by on the other side, he was drawn towards them by the strong, magnetic attraction of pure Christian love.

No other power in the world could have
held John so true to his cause and so loyal to
the African, whom he longed to serve, as this
magnet of the love of Christ.

Arthur Cripps, his friend, the poet and
evangelist, saw all this with the eyes of a
seer.   His verse, aflame with love for the
African, can hardly contain the hidden fires
within as he pictures his Lord and Master,
Jesus Christ, in Africa as One Whom he dares
to call the " Black Christ."   He cries in his
soul's agony :—

" *To me, as one born out of his due time,*
To me, as one not much to reckon in,
He hath revealed Himself, not as to Paul,

> *Christ, throned and crowned,*
> *But marred, despised, rejected,*
> *The Divine Outcast of a terrible land,*
> *The Black Christ, with parched lips and*
>   *empty hand."*

And again he writes, with an anguish so deep that it rends his own spirit,

> *No orb hath He, nor ring,*
> *No crown, nor throne.*
>   *Like worm, and like no man,*
> *They use him.*
>   *God forgive me, should I fail*
> *This Christ, thus robed, in bronze*
>   *or black, to hail!*

The burning fire within, which went to the composition of those lines, John also felt in his heart of hearts, though he had no power to express it in great English verse like his friend Arthur. But every day that he lived in Southern Rhodesia and saw the tragedy happening, before his eyes, of a disinherited people, the iron entered deeper and deeper into his soul.

At the same time we find John penitent and full of regrets that he had not been able to do more to make the meaning of his

Lord's command understood by his European fellow-countrymen. For, in Christ, they were equally dear to him, and he dreaded the thought of losing his balance and becoming one-sided.

" Oftentimes," he writes, " I felt deeply that the European settlers in this colony needed more of my attention. It was not that I underrated the importance of the work which was being carried on among them : it was simply lack of time and energy.

" The strain of the varied task I was attempting was very great. Right through, I had a sense of Divine strengthening and guidance. The Master Builder was God."

John longed to be a true peace-maker : to be able to interpret one race to the other without any bitterness or ill-feeling. But injustice towards the weak and defenceless roused at once within his nature such a passionate protest on behalf of the oppressed that his words became like fire.

This passion was mistaken for hostility by those who were hostile to John already, and they answered with heated language in return. Indeed, they came to regard him as " racially " biased on the African side and openly charged him with unfairness towards his own countrymen.

They did not understand that his love for his own country and his own countrymen was passionate also, and that he loved them no less than he loved the African whom he had come to serve in Christ's name.

It is not without deep significance that Christ marks out, in His beatitudes, the peacemakers as blessed, and goes on to say that they have the blessing of being called " God's children." For in a divine manner, as true children of their Heavenly Father, they have to suffer hostility from both sides, even as God, our Father, suffers and forgives with love.

For Jesus explains His own paradox concerning this " blessing " of the peacemakers and the persecuted when He says :

" Love your enemies ; do good to them that hate you, and pray for those that despitefully use you and persecute you ; that ye may be the children of your Father, which is in heaven. For He maketh His sun to shine upon the evil and the good, and sendeth His rain upon the just and the unjust. . . . Ye, therefore, shall be perfect, even as your Father in heaven is perfect."

" Blessed," says Jesus, " are the peacemakers : for they shall be called the children of God."

How John longed to win that blessing is plainly visible all through his life. It did not come naturally to him ; for he was a born fighter, and herein lay his great fundamental strength ; but this natural gift of character had to be tempered through and through, as steel is tempered, before it could bear the strain and become like the passion of his Master " who was led as a lamb to the slaughter and as a sheep before her shearers is dumb so opened He not His mouth," who, " when He was reviled, reviled not again ; when He suffered, threatened not ; but committed Himself to Him that judgeth righteously : who His own self bare our sins in His own body on the tree . . . by whose stripes ye were healed."[1]

---

[1] 1 Peter ii. 23, 24.

CHAPTER XIX : JOHN'S HUMOUR

VERY many stories about John's experiences in Rhodesia have been handed down, full of humour and pathos, and it may be well to break the narrative at this point and tell some of them in this book.

These stories, which John treasured, do much to reveal the kindly nature of the African folk among whom he lived and worked. They also illustrate many traits in John's character, where it approached theirs most closely. In these things the whole world is made kin. For the Africans who listen to these stories enjoy their kindly good humour just as much as we do ourselves.

Fortunately the record of most of the incidents that follow was given by John himself, so that we can almost hear his laugh and watch the twinkle in his eyes as he bubbled over with fun while he told them. Some of the best of them refer to the marriage ceremonies which John, whenever possible, liked to conduct. Here he was a true father of his people, teaching the young couples many useful lessons.

" People who turn to God," he relates,
" after taking a wife according to African
custom, are required by the Church, before
admission to full membership, to have a
Christian ceremony and take a monogamous
vow. Generally, for a wedding a small fee
is paid, to cover the cost of registration,
etc.

" At this station there were a number of
people who were not availing themselves of
the privilege of full membership, and I spoke
to them about it. ' Well,' they said, ' the
cost of the wedding is too much for us.'

" Very foolishly, we think, they go in for a
costly wedding—for them at any rate—by
purchasing materials for dresses, and by purchasing boots which they could not obtain in
Rhodesia at less than £1 to £1 10s. ; and for
many of them, this is the only time in their
lives that boots are worn. This they do
solely to imitate the white people.

" Now, when I mentioned this question of
full membership and they said they could
not afford the cost, I replied, ' Well, there is
one way in which I can help you : if you will
agree not to purchase boots for the wedding,
we will forgo the wedding fee. You need
pay nothing to the missionary and the
evangelist who officiate.'

"They went away to think over this proposal.

"A few days later, some members of the would-be wedding party came along to my house and said, 'The words you spoke the other day about forgoing the wedding fee, if we refrain from buying boots, will help us. We presume that you will also forgo the fee if we *borrow* the boots ?'

"Well, I thought their astuteness was worth a little consideration, and they passed through the ordeal without payment!"

A second story of a wedding, which always caused great merriment when he told it, runs thus :

"I had to go on one occasion to perform a marriage at one of my outside stations. There was quite a nice company of people gathered to witness the ceremony. A number of very bright girls, companions to the one who was being married, were there.

"It happened that this girl was very hysterical, and apparently, the excitement of being married brought on one of these attacks. So she was perturbed, and began to cry in such a manner that made it impossible for her to follow the ceremony and take any part in the responses.

"I stopped, and urged her to stop weeping,

to control her emotion, or we could not proceed with the ceremony. The poor thing made a desperate attempt to stop crying, but alas, she failed, and the crying began again.

" I had been told that in cases of hysteria, harsh treatment is the kindest and most effectual, so I stopped again, and with a twinkle in my eye which the congregation, at any rate, saw, I said to the audience, ' If this girl won't stop crying, then I must get one of these other girls, who are so full of smiles, to occupy her place, and she must go to the back of the church.'

" This certainly gave her a shock, and she pulled herself together, so that we got through the service. Then came the signing of the register after the ceremony was over.

" This signing of the register, which takes place in the church, is rather a formidable affair; contracting parties, who write very, very slowly, must write their names three times. I said to the teacher, ' While we are doing this, let the choir sing one of your school songs.'

" These good people know English very imperfectly, and learn the words by heart. To my amusement they struck up a song, the music of which they knew, ' When the storms of life are ended.' In the words of the chorus they got a bit mixed up.

" After they had gone on with this for some time, I said, ' Now we will have a change ; try something that is a bit brighter.' Again I was greatly amused at the choice. It was, ' John Brown's body lies a-mouldering in the tomb ! '

" These were not quite marriage songs, but they filled the place, and we got through all right."

A third story goes back before the marriage stage to that of courtship.

" At Waddilove," John said, " we have co-education, and a few strict rules have to be laid down concerning the relationship of the boys and girls. One is, that no letters must pass between them.

" I was walking up to the school one day when the scholars were leaving, and I saw a young man hand two letters to some girls who were passing out. I called the three and made them hand the letters to me, and I said to the young man, ' Now, Hofica, you must come along to see me a little later.'

" I read the letters. They were the usual type : the writer declared his undying love, and said terrible consequences would come to him if it was not reciprocated. The sender's real name was left out.

" I had to punish the young man, and gave him a job of cutting firewood for two days.

" On the second day, I happened to be passing where he was at work. I stopped, and said to him, ' I am very sorry for you, but you must learn to keep the rules of this school.' ' Now,' I continued, ' tell me who wrote the other letter.'

" ' I wrote both,' he said.

" ' But, Hofica,' I said, ' you are a Christian man. and you know that in the Christian Church polygamy is not allowed.'

" ' Yes, Minister,' he replied, ' but when a man plants his corn, he never knows where the seed will come up ! ' "

We turn now to a story told concerning one who had just come out from home to work in the mission field. It gives a vivid picture of what it means to go on tour in a village district in Mashonaland. The experience is not by any means confined to Africa.

" When one gets away," John relates, " from European centres and travels about amongst the villages, one finds the Africans very hospitable and kind. What they have they give freely. From a moral standard it is often crude.

Nothing pleased John so much as to tell a good story against himself. This short story which follows he thoroughly enjoyed.

" I went," he said, " one day to a heathen village to see the people and hold a service. They knew nothing, of course, about our forms of worship and about the God of whom we spoke and to whom we prayed.

" To people like that, I find the best appeal is through human relationships—God is a Father, and we are His children. As a Father, God's care for us : as children, our obedience. This is the relationship they may understand, and it was about these things that I talked that morning.

" ' Now,' I said, ' let us all kneel down and thank God for His love and for His benefits showered upon us.'

" I ought to explain that these people wear no boots and therefore move about noiselessly. We knelt in prayer ; in five minutes I had finished. What was my surprise to find, when I opened my eyes, that my congregation had vanished !

" In their superstition, they were afraid, and so they decamped ! "

Miss Marjorie Hudson, one of his staff at Nengubo, writes about John : " He was an inveterate tease. He would tease us till we were literally in tears and then stand with his hands on his sides shaking with laughter until you could do nothing but share in it and forget your wrath.

" He became a real chum, who, in spite of his age, had never lost the adventurous spirit of childhood and could enjoy a good long tramp over the veld, climb a kopje and revel in a picnic with the youngest of us.

" Everyone knew what good company he could be and what a fund of stories he had to suit every occasion. I have very vivid memories still of a first camp with him, how he kept us thrilled for hours one night round the fire telling stories of his early days in Rhodesia.

" He could keep cheery under all kinds of difficulties. He used to go out very early in the morning each day and would call in just as we finished breakfast. We might have been terribly cross before he came in, but his fun would put us right for the day.

" Sometimes I've seen him when we got stuck in the mud out on the veld. He would treat it all as a tremendous joke. Then, when it was all over, he would say with a smile, ' You know, there's nothing makes me so angry as to get stuck like that ! '

" He was perfectly *dreadful* in the way he

would take the car over the most impossible ground ! I've got in my mind a picture of how, one day, he had found a new road across country to a village where we were starting a new school. John White was driving the car.

"We came to a horrible little stream. It seemed quite mad to go on any farther, but he popped out, had one good look at it and popped in again, saying, ' Oh ! this is nothing ! ' and off we went. We bumped into an awful hole in the middle and the car seemed to be turning upside down, but of course we got through.

"That was typical of the way he would go at a difficult situation, without a scrap of fear. Someone said the other day, ' You need John White here to tackle this. He would have revelled in it ! '

"He was very patient with the Mashona people. He would talk round and round some little matter for hours at a stretch, until he had won them. But where their rights were concerned, or whenever he thought they were being unjustly treated, he used a sledge-hammer ! "

On another occasion a man and his wife came to John. The husband said, " My wife wants her tooth extracted." John took a good look and performed the operation to her great satisfaction.

The man then said to John, " I want one out also ! "

" Well ! " said John, with a laugh, " You *are* a brave fellow, you are ! to send your wife to have her tooth out first ! "

" Not at all," said the man, " I wanted to see how much skill you had from what you did to my wife ! "

John had an old jam-tin fitted up with a hole in the top and used to invite them to put in a threepenny-bit for the sake of the orphans of the Mission in order to give them a chance to show their gratitude to God for the deliverance from pain that they experienced owing to his simple medical treatment.

The next story carries a deep pathos with it and is nearer to tears than laughter.

" At a village," John tells us, " some four miles from my home there lived for many years a native named Jack Shamu. When I first went to this place, he heard of the kind of work we were doing, and came to see us to enquire if he could get a place on which to live and cultivate food for his family. Having got this permission, he gathered his family together and trekked to his new abode.

" He was then a middle-aged man. There was little possibility of him availing himself of the school, and so he remained to the end of his days unable to read, but he came occasionally to church, and subscribed, for him, liberally towards the support of an evangelist.

" His work at his own home was chiefly looking after his cattle until two years ago, when blindness began to creep over his eyes. Nothing could be done for him, and the poor old man was very much troubled. Periodically he used to come to my house, led by one of his children, and we chatted together about all kinds of things. I used to help him to sell his cattle and looked after his money. In these matters he trusted me without reserve.

" In February, 1932, we were leaving for home and I went over to his village to bid him good-bye. Jack Shamu was deeply affected. He enumerated the services that I had rendered to him, and then he said : ' These things that you have done for me are good things, but the greatest service that you have rendered was to teach me to pray. When I was alone on the veld, where everything was quiet, I there talked to the great God, and this has helped me greatly.'

" On our departure from that country we had many testimonies of the value of our work, but nothing pleased me more than these simple words from this man."

The last three stories were not told by John himself, but by African Christians who loved him so dearly because he knew exactly where the " shoe pinched " in their own lives. They had come suddenly under the new control of the European and they hardly, as yet, understood what they ought to do. John sympathised with them in their difficulties and sometimes got into trouble himself for doing so.

" Since the rebellion," one of these stories runs, " Africans have not been allowed to carry firearms, although in the early days the cattle and the goats used to be worried by lions and leopards and the baboons used to destroy their gardens.

" There lived at a village four miles from Epworth an evangelist named James Kamera, whose goats were suffering from the raids of a leopard. He came to John White, begging him to help.

" John White thought for a moment and then said : ' The law does not permit you to carry a gun, and you'll have to suffer the loss.'

" ' Can you come and help shoot the leopard ? ' asked Kamera.

" ' I should have to wait a very long time,' said John White, ' for that leopard to return. But though the law does not permit you to carry a gun I will help you by lending you a gun, but you must take care of it and keep it out of sight.'

" James took it to his house and there came to him one day two Europeans, and on seeing the gun in the house, they reported the matter to the police, and as the result of the case James Kamera was fined £10 and John White was fined £10, and also lost his rifle, which was very valuable. All as the result of trying to help in a time of need ! "

Another good story, showing John's kindly nature, runs thus :

" Nengubo farm is near the Native Reserve, and the cattle belonging to natives in the Reserve used to stray into the Mission lands and do damage. The people who owned them were warned again and again, but they did not take any notice.

" The man in charge of looking after the farm gardens asked permission to ' pound ' them, which meant to say that they would be driven into Marandellas and kept there until the owners claimed them. The owners,

before they were given the cattle, would have
to pay the expenses.

" So John White reluctantly agreed that
the cattle should be sent.

" When the cattle had been driven for
about a mile or two, the owners came beseeching him to give them their cattle back again ;
for the cost of getting the cattle back again
to the kraal would have been about five
pounds.

" John White looked at these beseeching
people and smiled. He then called a boy
and bade him run after the herdboy driving
the cattle and tell him to restore the cattle
to their owners, on the promise that they
would not allow them to stray again."

The last story to be told about John is
perhaps the most quaintly humorous of all,
if we picture the incident to ourselves. And
what a perfect trust it shows on the part of
those concerned ! It also shows the long-
suffering of the Mashona people and their
power of endurance.

" One day a native policeman arrested a
native in the Chihota Reserve. He made
the prisoner carry all his blankets and food.

" The policeman was riding a cycle and he
made the prisoner run by the side of his cycle
for six miles. By this time they had reached

Waddilove Mission and John White happened
to see them, so he stopped them and asked
the policeman why he was making the man
run.

" The policeman replied, that if he did not
make the man run, he himself would be three
hours late and would get punished. He
therefore intended making the prisoner run
for the rest of the distance, which was about
thirteen miles.

" Not wishing the policeman to get into
trouble and also feeling for the native who
had to run with such a heavy load, John got
out his motor-car and took them both to
Marandellas, tying the policeman's cycle on
the side of the car ! "

This chapter may well be concluded with
the contrast drawn by John himself between
what he saw more than thirty years ago when
he went through the Chihota Reserve and
what he met with on his last journey before
going back to England for the last time. All
the Christian love and kindly good humour
of John had borne fruit and won the hearts
of simple people like those with whom he had
to deal. The Gospel had won its way.

" More than thirty years ago," John writes,
" I passed through Chihota Reserve with a
few Mashona companions ; our approach to

the villages was not hailed with any delight ;
we were an entirely foreign element to them.
We found the villages in an indescribably
dirty condition, the people practically unclad.
At our approach, they ran away for shelter.
The adults were suspicious, sullen, un-
friendly ; night was made hideous by their
dances and drunken revelry. If the crops
were good, plentiful supplies of beer were
forthcoming.

" I was then very imperfectly acquainted
with African life, but quickly came to the
conclusion that paganism had little that was
good to say for itself. These poor people
were objects of pity. Had Jesus been on
that trip with me, He would have wept, as
He did over Jerusalem. One felt, too, that we
Christians had something to help them greatly.

" That is a very brief picture of what kind
of things I met more than thirty years ago.
I want you to look at the contrast.

" Before starting out for home at the
beginning of last year, we went to bid farewell to our African friends. At every place
the community welcomed us with shouts of
pleasure. The middle-aged people were the
youths and maidens of our first trip. We
were friends, and talked familiarly together.
Services were conducted in the churches,

which were generally full of people. They were now dressed in fairly good clothing and had a clean, tidy appearance. The villages now were mostly cleaned up and had altogether a better appearance. The houses were larger and more suited to civilised people. One could not but exclaim as one passed through this country, ' What great things hath God wrought ! ' "

CHAPTER XX : THE SIGNS OF THE TIMES

WHILE John White and Arthur Cripps stood out together more and more decisively as the champions of the African people, a line of division began to mark them off from other missionaries, including the Bishop of Southern Rhodesia, Dr. Paget.

This came about very gradually, and at first no one wished to acknowledge it, or make it public ; for it was obviously of vital consequence that all should work together.

The difference was one of degree. The two friends, John and Arthur, were regarded as more uncompromising than the rest in their attitude towards the Government, and therefore less acceptable to the officials on the one hand and the European settlers on the other. At the same time, it would be true to say that no two missionaries knew the African mind as these two knew it.

" I think it can be safely said," writes L. P Hardaker, the Secretary of the Missionary Conference, " that no act affecting African life ever became law in Southern Rhodesia without John White having something to

say on it.   In the early days he stood almost
alone.   He and his friend, Arthur Cripps,
were outstanding figures for many years in
the fight for the removal of any racial injustice
from the African natives."

Naturally, in his struggle on behalf of
those who could not help themselves, they
became marked men.   They could neither be
silenced, nor yet be ignored.   But they were
regarded by most Europeans as impossible
extremists.   The two friends kept close together and in touch with one another through
regular weekly correspondence.   They seldom
took action without previous consultation.
John then would put forward his case with
such telling effect and merciless logic, that
he made for himself many enemies.   Some
of these became most bitter in their denun-
ciation of him.   He always regretted this
when it happened, for he was the enemy of
none and bore no resentment.   But he would
never tone down anything which he felt to
be a true statement of the facts.

" As secretary," L. P. Hardaker continues,
" I was closely associated with him for ten
years.   He could always realise more quickly
than others what the effect on the African
natives would be of any proposed measure.
For they came to him more than to anyone

else, and they poured into his ears their stories of ill-treatment or injustice. They were always sure of a sympathetic hearing from John White.

" He often said to me that his name was like a ' red rag to a bull ' in certain European quarters ; and I think in later years he kept his own name out of public agitation, whenever possible, for this reason. In case, however, there was some matter which he thought ought to be raised, he never hesitated for a moment. No amount of ill-favour or opposition could ever deter him."

On different occasions, when John's and Arthur's united interference had led to large and substantial modifications of the Government policy, after it had been declared, the dislike of the European settlers at what was called "parsons meddling in politics," became very pronounced, and these two friends, who had conspired together in this manner, were called upon to bear the brunt of it.

Very few Europeans were ready to cast a slur on their characters or to impugn their motives, which were quite above suspicion ; for the hardship and self-sacrifice of their lives were acknowledged by all. But the opinion was very widely held that their persistent advocacy on behalf of the African was stirring up serious unrest among the Mashona, and that it might even lead on in the end to another rebellion. This vague fear, which was constantly at the back of the settlers' hostile attitude, accounted for much of the bitter prejudice which some of John's actions created in the minds of his opponents.

One special mode of attack which he adopted, most of all incensed the Europeans. He would continually appeal over their heads to the newspaper press in England and to the Colonial Office. This was, to the settlers, an unpardonable offence. For they were intensely jealous of what they regarded as their " right " to legislate for the natives of the country.

This "right" John would never for a moment concede. He declared that so long as the voting power was almost wholly European, they could not be said to represent those who had no · franchise. The British Parliament was the court of appeal and he was determined on behalf of the Mashona people to claim that right.

Just before the Missionary Conference of 1928, at Salisbury, of which he was Chairman, this bitterness came to a head. Salisbury is the capital of Southern Rhodesia. The Mayor refused to attend the Conference because

John White was in the chair. For John had recently written to the English papers about the whole question of trusteeship for the Africans in such a manner as to offend deeply the Europeans.

But not only had there been strong disapprobation of the Conference Chairman's actions on the part of those outside, there had also been trouble within the ranks of the Conference itself. For objection had been taken to the Chairman inviting the help of the " Aborigines and Anti-Slavery Society," in London, in order to defeat a measure which made legal the compulsory indenture of young African boys found loafing in industrial centres. The word " child-slavery" had been applied to this new legislation by the British newspapers. Missionary opinion was itself divided about the Bill, some missionaries regarding it as necessary, and therefore looking upon such harsh criticism of it in London by the Anti-Slavery Society as essentially unfair, while others sided with John and Arthur and were ready to resist it to the uttermost.

This internal dissension, which must have been exceedingly painful to both sides of the Missionary Conference, made plain at last to the outside world that within the Executive of the Conference itself there was a very sharp division of opinion on a vital subject.

The Bishop, who took the side of the Government authorities, had written to a prominent Rhodesian newspaper, whose circulation was chiefly in one of the mining districts, as follows :

" I ask, is this Act for the enrichment and development of the African peoples, or is it for their exploitation ? I say emphatically that, to me, its intention is the former, and therefore to the glory of God."

This letter came as a terrible blow to John White, and at first he tried to avoid an open breach through the press. His own knowledge of the Mashonas was far more intimate and of far longer standing than that of the Bishop. Indeed, he had been in the country thirty years longer than Dr. Paget. Therefore he was able to detect latent evils of which the Bishop was entirely unaware.

In the end, John felt that a public answer was necessary, and he wrote to the press as follows :

" The intention of the Administration was, I believe, to make the Bill beneficial both to the employers and employed. But, surely, there may be two opinions as to how far they have succeeded.

" That a very undesirable state of things exists owing to the flocking of these juveniles to our industrial centres cannot be seriously questioned. If the effect of contact with our civilisation on the character of adults has been bad, how much worse must it be on these mere children !

" Now, what is to be the remedy ? Major Hudson admits that these juveniles often leave home without the consent of their parents. Surely, the wise and proper thing is to send them home and thus strengthen parental authority. Neither whipping, nor indenturing, will help in the desired direction if they are left in those dangerous circumstances to which they have apparently succumbed.

" We are told of one mine where fifty per cent. of the labour is juvenile ! Let me ask of those who have experienced its dangers, if the congregating of such a number of undisciplined youths is a wise arrangement ?

" We are told that the mothers are being rationed by the mine authorities to keep the boys there. Yet the better-class African people have again and again protested against their women-folk being allowed to leave their homes and their husbands in order that they may resort to such compounds. . . . The conditions of our kraals are not ideal, but I would much prefer to see the children grow up there, happy and irresponsible as children should be, than bound and fettered in our rigid industrial machine—polish and regulate it how you may. That will come ; but for the future of the African race's sake, don't force the pace ! "

Arthur Cripps, writing to the *Manchester Guardian,* and quoting both these letters, ends his own statement in this characteristic manner :

" Is this child-labour measure likely to promote the glory of God ? I trow not. My own view is that this binding of young children in tight civil contracts, which can be enforced by such criminal penalties as recall those of pre-Abolition days, threatens the South Rhodesian African with a form of child slavery."

Since the time when this controversy took place, the Act has become a dead letter. One can easily recognise to-day the serious dangers which such a method of administration in Southern Rhodesia might have involved if it had not been stopped at the outset by bringing to bear against it the full weight of world public opinion. Instead of discouraging child labour, which had already reached alarming proportions because of its comparative cheapness, it would have tended to encourage it, and thus have brought down the whole status of the adult African workman in Southern Rhodesia.

When the Missionary Conference of 1928 at Salisbury had opened in this heated and disturbed atmosphere, a fine thing happened. The Bishop of Southern Rhodesia himself, who had always been a great admirer of John White, even while disagreeing with his actions, brought forward a resolution proposing a " standing " vote of appreciation for the high services rendered to the country by the two missionaries, John White and Arthur Cripps.   It ran as follows : " That the Conference wishes to place on record its high appreciation of the services to their country of the missionaries who have received heavy criticism of late. Such criticism from any of our members does not cancel our recognition of their high and noble services to the country and its people, African and European."

The vote was carried standing, and John White briefly replied.

Then, as Chairman of the Conference, he read one of the most impressive addresses he had ever delivered, dealing with " The Signs of the Times."

He began with a warm tribute to the sympathy of the Director of Education who had assisted the missionaries in their difficult work to the utmost of his power.

Apart from much that was encouraging in this and in other respects, there were signs of the times, John said, that were very disconcerting indeed.

One of the most ominous of these signs of the times was the fact that, in spite of all the efforts which had been made for the furtherance of Christ's kingdom in a pagan world, where evil was rampant, the Churches had not even kept pace with the natural growth of the population to the south of the Zambesi. What was even more disconcerting was this, that the fair flowers of the Christian corporate life which ought to be blossoming within the Christian Church—contentment, good-will, justice, temperance, righteousness—were still struggling for their very existence owing to the racial hostility which had invaded the sanctuary of God itself.

" No nation," John declared with solemn warning, " can long survive that is torn by distrust, dissension and racial prejudice of the worst type."

In Christ Jesus alone. he went on, lay the

one supreme answer to all the gravest difficulties which threatened their own missionary
work.

" It was either Christ or catastrophe for
Rhodesia."

But the first duty of all which every
missionary had to face was to examine his
own personal life. Were they themselves
entirely free from blame with regard to the
racial prejudices, superstitions and misunder-
standings which were keeping men out of the
Kingdom of God and putting Christ to open
shame ?

On two vital matters this examination
might proceed :

(1) Was the emphasis correct in the
message they gave ?   The sin-weary, witch-
bound, heathen African needed to know
Christ as the Saviour and Deliverer, who
could give him the joyful freedom of a
true son of God. That was the primary
message.

(2) But there was needed a further
message of Christ the Fulfiller and Upbuilder
to complete the work of deliverance.

Did they recognise this, John asked, or
did they stop short ? No one could read
Stanley Jones's book, *The Christ of the Indian
Road*, without realising in his heart the need

for the true missionary to go the "other mile," and show that the Christian Gospel had a message for the corporate as well as the individual needs of those he came out to help. He must not be afraid of nationalism, and all that it implied. Why should he? Did not Jesus number among His own disciples one called Simon the Zealot?

John, as Chairman of the Conference, then went forward to deal from this angle of vision with the most difficult question of all, namely, the relation between the two races in Southern Rhodesia *within the One Body of Christ.*

"This relationship," he said, "is now clearly understood by the African people. They are aware that we use the same Name, read the same Bible, sing the same hymns, kneel at the same table of Holy Communion. . . . As, Sunday by Sunday, there arises to Heaven in our sanctuaries the great prayer, ' Thy kingdom come,' inevitably the Africans ask, ' Do these Christians who come from Europe mean what they say? Do they mean God's kingdom as Christ meant it? In its great sweep does it include the African multitudes who dwell at the door of the West? ' That is a question which needs an honest answer."

John mentioned with thankfulness a letter
that he had just received from the Rand, in
the Transvaal, where some young Europeans
had been led to take part in the African
religious services conducted in the mining
compounds.

This letter from an African Christian had
run : " When I thought this over I said to
myself, ' Really these people have a great
love for the Africans. This has shown me
that Christ really rules in these European
hearts.' "

On the other hand, one of the African
Christians had bitterly said, " The Church
that I see around me has drifted from Christ's
teaching, and sided with the rich against the
poor."

He concludes with a passage which con-
tains wrapped up in it some of the deepest
convictions of a lifetime. It cannot be
abridged, but must be quoted here in full :

" We are being constantly reminded," he
says, " and most people believe it, that the
outstanding problem, whether social, economic
or political, confronting South Africa to-day,
is a racial one. What is the Church's con-
tribution towards its solution ? " At the heart
of all these questions is a great moral issue.
We cannot excuse ourselves by saying, " This

is a political affair." The Church cannot relegate its function of moral leadership to another. When it does that, it proclaims its own bankruptcy. Thus says the courageous author of *The Impatience of a Parson.* "The time has come," this writer asserts, "when our countrymen must say whether they desire Christianity to prevail, or whether they must frankly confess that it is too hard a way."

"Has the Church of God," John asks, "nothing to say about the action of its City Councillors in passing a ' colour bar ' resolution in its most objectionable form ?

"Has the Church in South Africa nothing to suggest for the relief of the large crowd of underpaid, often ill-housed, unskilled workers, who toil for us and contribute so substantially to the prosperity of the country ?

"Has the Church no advice concerning the deplorable position of the large landless multitude of Africans, whose cry is constantly sounding in our ears ?

"Is it not for the Church to point the more excellent way out of the present tangle of racial passions and selfish interests, so as to blaze the path that leads to a larger and freer life, to ally ourselves with every movement that makes for conciliation, co-operation, contentment, and a wider prosperity ?

"The Church must stand for idealism against compromise and panic legislation. The way that I point to is no flowery path of ease. It leads to the heights. It means hard climbing all the way.

"It is the way our Leader went: it is the way of the Cross."

When this eventful conference was over, and John White went back to Waddilove, he knew that a change was taking place which was really an inward call to him to give way to younger men. He was already drawing nearer to the three score years and ten about which the Psalmist has spoken, and deep within his physical frame he had begun to experience the first symptoms of a long-drawn pain from which there was to be no escape. In a sense, the same test of discipleship had already come close to his own brave spirit which the Lord Jesus had laid upon His disciple, Simon Peter.

"When thou wast young," the Master had said, "thou girdedst thyself and walkedst whither thou wouldest; but when thou shalt be old, thou shalt stretch forth thy hands, and another shall gird thee, and carry thee whither thou wouldest not."

For physical infirmity had already begun to give its own inner warning. Only in the silence of the night was the dim apprehension of what he might in the end be called upon to bear brought home to him. It was mingled, in the closing years of his missionary work, with mental and spiritual distress which in its discipline of pain must have prepared him beforehand for the months of physical suffering which were to follow.

What that mental distress was the next chapter will disclose.

THE Missionary Conference at Salisbury in 1928, over which John White had presided with such distinction, had revealed only too clearly to those who were able to read the signs of the times the rift which was every day growing wider and separating Arthur Cripps and himself from other missionaries with whom John always sought to work on cordial terms.

His one great fear at this time was that the missionary force in Southern Rhodesia as a whole might lose its sturdy strength and independence. Educational funds were being distributed by Government as " grants-in-aid," and it was easy, with these grants always in mind, to be influenced unduly by Government on questions vitally affecting the welfare of the African people.

John felt quite certain that any close alliance between the missionaries and the Administration would be fatal. It would be certain to end, he thought, in selling their birthright of independence for a mess of pottage. The African people would rightly begin to suspect their good faith, and the Christian religion itself, which preached unworldliness, would be compromised by their actions.

The two friends, John and Arthur, had puzzled together for a very long time over this tangled and complicated question. Arthur, as a free-lance, had gone so far in rejection of grants-in-aid as to carry on mission schools at his own expense. Though the cost had been almost prohibitive and the schools had been poor in equipment, nevertheless his spiritual liberty had been preserved intact. John deeply admired Arthur's courage in thus maintaining his freedom, but he could never bring himself to accept the same position.

Logically he might wish to act in the same manner as Arthur, but his essentially practical mind was always working towards a wider solution. As the trusted friend of the Mashonas, he had attempted to build up the whole missionary body in Southern Rhodesia into an active and powerful organisation, which should stand out on behalf of the African people in all vital concerns. He hoped to be able to make this body so effective that the Rhodesian Administration on the spot, and the Secretary of State for the

Colonies in London would recognise and respect its judgments to such an extent as to seek its advice on all critical occasions. He attempted further to establish the convention of employing the executive of this Missionary Conference, as a standing Committee, to deal with important interim questions that might arrive while the Conference was not in session.

The fact must be remembered that the whole future status of the Mashona people depended on what was decided in these fateful years. Since there was no special party of Europeans in the Rhodesian Legislature elected for the purpose of supporting African interests, John sought, with immense patience and foresight, to make the Conference itself fulfil that function.

It was a great and noble conception, suited to the special time in which he carried on his work. Indeed, for some years things happened in the very way that John himself had so ably planned. The Conference was respected by the Administration, which always sent one of its own officials to be present as a listener when African affairs were discussed. On all such vital matters as land, taxation, health, education, etc., the Conference had a powerful voice and what it proposed reached England through the columns of the press.

But there were always two special dangers which stood in the way, either of which might at any time wreck the whole scheme.

The first of these has already been mentioned. The independence of the Missionary Conference and its executive might be sapped by the Administration withdrawing its grants. Even if no definite bargain was struck, a mutual agreement might be formed which would undermine the independence of the missionary side. For the coarse maxim of modern politics might at any time be cited that "he who pays the piper calls the tune."

So far had compromise already gone in this matter that the sudden withdrawal of a Government educational grant was a serious prospect that no mission superintendent in Southern Rhodesia could contemplate without misgiving. This increasing dependence in Government grants tended to weaken united action of the missionary body when ever it was necessary to oppose Government policy.

The second obstacle that stood in John's way was the persistent refusal on the part of some missionaries to participate in any political endeavour, even on behalf of the

Africans, at a time when there was no one else to help them in their trouble.

These good men, who were entirely occupied with the direct preaching of the Gospel, were afraid of taking even a single step forward in the direction of what they felt to be political activity. Their position has already been discussed and need not detain us here.[1] But it will easily be understood what active opposition men of this character might offer to any use of the Missionary Conference as a political factor in African native affairs.

These two difficulties which John encountered were, of course, not confined to missionary work in Southern Rhodesia. They are felt acutely in almost every country where Government seeks the aid of missions, and vice versa. Especially, in the twentieth century, they are being experienced in Central Africa, for it has become a matter of practical administration by different Governments to entrust African education to missionary hands. It is in reality the old division between " Church " and " State " in a new form. The pages of history are strewn with the wreckage of different attempts to adjust such relations.

[1] See chapter xviii, p. 197.

Therefore it was on no minor or secondary issue that John disagreed with his fellow missionaries. At Salisbury he felt that things he valued most of all were at stake. The whole future of the Missionary Conference was threatened by the diverse and opposite convictions held on these matters.

After the Conference, John returned to England and met Arthur Cripps. The latter writes about this meeting with John : " I saw John White in England not long after the Missionary Conference, and I think, from what I remember of him then, that he had been wounded in the house of his friends."

In the bracing climate of England John's health seemed to improve a little, and he soon threw off this disappointment, for he was always cheerful by nature, and divine grace had added a faculty of rejoicing even in the midst of tribulations. He returned with Mrs. White to Southern Rhodesia in 1929.

In a short statement of his own called " Looking Backward," he has summed up the events that followed in the next two years :

" With the work," he writes, " growing on every side, I felt it impossible to continue in the different offices I had held. I was Chairman of the District, Principal of Waddilove, Superintendent of Nengubo Circuit, and also in charge of the Book Room, which distributed literature to all the circuits in the district. Clearly this could not go on. What must I relinquish ? I felt that the choice was largely with me.

" The Chairmanship tried my strength very much. So I decided to ask for my release from it. I was succeeded by the Rev. Frank Noble, who in five years has shown himself a very capable administrator.

" The Waddilove Institution had grown both in size and importance, and it seemed wise to appoint another principal for that.

" But my health was still failing, and it soon became apparent that I must seek surgical aid. This I did, with only comparative success."

It is deeply touching to me to look back and remember that he never mentioned to me (while I was with him at a later date) his own disappointments during the last years of his ministry in Southern Rhodesia. He would surely have done so if there had still been any burden on his mind, for he told me everything as a friend. But during those marvellous months at Kingsmead Close the sunshine of God's love was again filling his whole life with gladness, and the distress of those years had been forgotten.

If, therefore, I mention untoward incidents at this place in my narrative it is in order to make clear that the same human weaknesses appear on the mission field in distant lands, which we know so well among ourselves. They are often most apparent where men and women live together, consecrated to a common work, calling for sacrifice, under a continual nervous tension.

John had the weaknesses due to impatience no less than others, and he was the first to acknowledge them.[1] But the beauty of his singularly noble character lay in this, that he overcame them, day by day, afresh as he entered into the secret of the presence of his Lord. Following in his Master's footsteps, he " learned obedience by the things that he suffered."[2] He looked away from himself to " Jesus, Who for the joy that was set before him endured the Cross despising the shame."[3]

Therefore, during those last radiant months, as the concluding chapters will reveal, the dark cloud had entirely vanished. The true Light was shining brightly again in every part of his sunny nature. He could say with the Apostle, " This, then, is the message which we have heard from Him and declare

[1] See p. 272.   [2] Heb. v. 8.   [3] Heb. xii. 3.

unto you, that God is Light and in Him is no darkness at all.''[1]

It is possible to find out from the records of the Conference in 1930 what actually happened.

Between 1928 and 1930 the differences between John and the other members of the Conference had come to a head. Arthur was away in England. John was alone. Younger men, who would have taken John's side, had not come forward into prominence during the discussions.

During the sessions he made a direct challenge to those who administered justice in Southern Rhodesia to the Mashona people. He pointed out how almost impossible it was to get a fair hearing, owing to the police methods of extracting evidence. No one knew these facts better than John White did, and he brought them fearlessly forward before the authorities on behalf of those whom he loved.

This direct challenge was taken up in a hostile manner by the Colonial Secretary, who was present as an invited guest. When John sat down the Government Secretary at once rose and rebuked him in a very pointed manner. John was probably the oldest

[1] 1 John i. 5.

missionary present, and this attack by the
Government official was surely uncalled for,
because the facts were well known.   But the
Conference remained silent.

John wrote to his friend Arthur in London
a pathetic letter describing what had
happened.

" I spoke," he wrote, " at the Conference
on the manner by which admissions were
obtained from African natives and urged that
there should be a restriction of the use of
such evidence.   The Colonial Secretary was
very angry and gave me a severe lecture.
Not a soul spoke a word in favour of what I
had said.   When the time came for the
election of the Executive, I was left out.   So
my reputation, I fear, is gone in missionary
circles.   About that I need not worry ! "

But John *did* worry.   He could not help
worrying.   His health was failing him.   His
" thorn in the flesh "—the internal disease—
was cruelly beginning to torment him.   Everything was continually going against him, and
he uttered that bitter cry which rings through
his letter to his friend.   It recalls the word of
Paul in his last struggle : " At my first answer
no man stood with me, but all forsook me."[1]

To John himself, at that dark moment of

[1] 2 Tim. iv. 16.

his life, it seemed like the betrayal of a great
cause. On that one issue of upholding the
true rights of the African he had staked all
that he had—his whole life, his reputation,
his fair name, everything he valued in the
world.

Arthur Cripps, his closest friend, in re-
lating this story, compares this " day of
darkness and defeat," when the enemy
triumphed, to the sad breaking up of the
noble companionship of the Order of the
Knights of the Round Table, which King
Arthur had formed at Lyonesse in order to
bring peace and righteousness down among
men. It meant, he said, that once more
confusion and disorder would return and the
fair earth would be " full of darkness and
cruel habitations."

When it is remembered how the Missionary
Conference of Southern Rhodesia had owed
its very existence to John White's persistent
sacrifice of time and energy, and also to his
high endeavour to make it a power for good
in the land, it can be seen how deep the
wound had gone when he found his name
omitted from the Executive. It meant for
him that he was now cut adrift from that
which had been a life work to him.

But even this blow did not fall alone during

the fateful year, 1930. In his simplicity of heart he had done what probably should never have been attempted. He remained on the spot, close to Waddilove, after handing over the chief command. Even if his health had been perfect, to remain at hand in those circumstances, when a new order of things was being tried out and a new policy was being pursued, had elements of danger in it which ought to have been avoided. But he did not seem to realise them at this time.

Waddilove meant everything to John. It was one of his own creations, almost like his own child. Suddenly to relinquish all control and yet remain, was surely a mistake which a simple, great-hearted man might make, but which was almost sure to lead to suffering. The burden of that year, as his strength decayed, had a terribly depressing effect upon him and added to his illness.

In the year 1931 he had become very seriously ill. An examination by the doctors revealed at last what was the real cause of his illness. Dr. Huggins was convinced that for a long time past he had been suffering from a malignant growth, or cancer, and that a successful operation was not likely to be possible because the disease was so deep-seated.

His last journey through Rhodesia was

very deeply touching. He was clearly very ill, however much he tried to make light of it ; and as he went from place to place the kindly African people who were devoted to him became instinctively aware that he might be unable to return. They might " see his face no more." [1] So they showered upon him their affection. Wherever he halted it was the same. They crowded round him to bid him farewell and to pray for his return if that might be the will of God.

To Mrs. White herself the facts had been made known, and she bore the news with splendid fortitude, seeking to remain cheerful for her husband's sake. For it had been decided to say nothing to him until the news had been confirmed by a special examination in London. Therefore, in her devotion to her husband, she had the pain of knowing before-hand the malignant character of the disease, while she was unable to say anything to him about the dread secret she carried with her.

Even amid the sadness of farewell and the weakness of his physical condition, John's humour did not fail him. The story is told by Kate Snel, of Bulawayo, how on the crowded day of leave-taking he came to the farewell social in the Methodist Hall and

[1] Acts xx. 38.

went up to Mrs. Maggie Squair and said in his genial manner :

" Well, how do you do, Mrs. Squair ? It's a long time since we've met, and it will be good-bye as well, I'm afraid, as we're on the way home."

" And hoo are ye the noo, Mr. White ? " said Maggie Squair, in broad Scotch.

" Noo sae bad," said John, trying to answer her in fun with her own Scotch accent. " Noo sae bad, ye ken. Juist joggin' along."

Kate Snel, who relates this simple story, goes on to say that the brave impression of good cheer left on her by this touch of humour, when he looked so haggard and ill, will remain with her to the end—a man indeed to be envied for his high courage ; striving to do his best to the utmost even in the most untoward circumstance. He had, in early days, faced the dangers of the roads from Mission to Mission in all weathers ; he had lived on scant food in African kraals ; meeting swollen rivers, roads full of ruts, and all the many obstacles that are hardly known in these modern days.

She relates how once in the old days he started his journey with only two slices of bread, saying, " It'll be plenty for me ! I'll find my food on the way as I go along."

And so with his characteristic humour

and cheery goodwill, she relates, he "found his food on the way" right up to the end.

On the voyage home he became worse, and he must have himself suspected that something was seriously wrong.

Then came the London examination at the Charing Cross Hospital, and Dr. Huggins's opinion was confirmed. The X-ray revealed that the cancer was so deep-seated that no major operation was possible.

All that could be done was to seek to relieve the pain after certain minor operations had been performed.

At this time of gloom and darkness in the outer things of life, it was a comfort and satisfaction to receive the following letter from the Department of Native Development, Salisbury, which remained among his treasured possessions in England during his long illness.

I cannot allow you to leave South Africa without an attempt, however inadequate it may be, to express something of what I feel concerning your great life-work in Southern Rhodesia. You have every reason to look back with pardonable pride upon what you have been able to accomplish in this territory in loyalty to the spiritual ideals you have consistently held and so effectively applied.

It is not given to many men to exercise so marked an influence in the forging of a new nation, since your long and arduous labours have synchronised with the unfolding of much significant history in the annals of the young colony.

That you have fearlessly held a watching brief for the emerging Africans is common knowledge ; that you have also helped to lay enduring foundations within your church and school system is also common knowledge. What you have done in the lives of so many African natives is best known to them and to the Master you led them to serve.

May I thank you on behalf of this Department of Native Development for your valuable assistance throughout our own difficult probationary period. You supplied us at once a stimulus and a challenge, and in spite of our mistakes you believed sufficiently in our endeavours to give us very real support. In addition, may I add my personal thanks for the gift of your friendship. . . .

Harold Jowitt.

Such a letter speaks volumes both for John himself and also for the authorities who were thus able to recognise his sterling merit and his outstanding sincerity of purpose.

CHAPTER XXII : THE SHADOW OF DEATH

In this chapter, as we reach the last days and the conclusion of our story, it is best wherever possible to let John speak for himself through some of the more personal letters which he wrote to friends both in England and Mashonaland.

He was now fully aware how serious his illness was, and realised that he was called upon to face the near approach of death in the spirit of his Lord and Master whom he loved to serve.

For a moment his brave spirit recoiled and he shrank back from the thought. The story is told by his life-long friend, the Rev. H. H. Whiting, to whom he had written nearly forty years before asking for his prayers on the night when he made the decision to trust his mother's health in God's hands and accept the call to go out to the mission field.[1]

" On his return home," writes Mr. Whiting, " after forty years of heroic toil, he looked forward to spending life's eventide among his friends, and going here and there, pleading for the work that was so dear to his heart. But when he realised the serious nature of

[1] See chapter III, p. 27.

the disease and that his days were numbered,
the shock at first was great, and once again
he asked me to pray for him.

" It was not long before he wrote these words,
' I want you to know that it is all right once
again.   I don't say that it has been easy for me,
for it has not ! But my Lord and I have once
more talked matters over, and He has told
me that He wants me for service above.' "

John never wrote easily or fluently his
letters to his friends.   They were composed
in quiet moments when he could think out
slowly each sentence which he wished to set
down.   Nor did he write much in these last
days.   I have often seen him composing
them, sentence by sentence, with pauses in
between.   Only when his correspondence was
concerned with business matters that needed
immediate attention had he "the pen of a ready
writer."   But he has put some of his deepest
thoughts into these last letters to his friends, and
the simple heart of a child is evident in them.

While reading them over, we get some
insight into his mind as he looks death full
in the face.   He turns at once to his Lord
and Master and he does not turn in vain.
The comfort comes which he so sorely needs.

It was not at all easy for him, with his
abundant zest for life, to realise at first all

that the doctors had told him and to reconcile himself to the fact that in all human probability he would never see his loved Mashona people again. As we shall see later, this one thought disturbed him more than any other—whether he was true to the promise he had given them that, if possible, he would die among them.

We can see him, in these letters, far away in distant England, with his heart aching to return. He receives and reads over again and again some precious letter that has come to him by the last mail from Epworth Farm, or Enkeldoorn, or Waddilove, in Mashonaland, and his eyes are filled with tears. His whole heart goes out across the sea and he seeks to put into a few sentences of love his longing for his friends.

" It *was* good," he writes to Frank Mussell, " to hear from you, dear comrade, by the last mail from South Africa. I am so glad to know that you like Epworth and enjoy the work there. You must not expect to find them all ' wings.' Some of them can be quite irritating. But patience and sympathy go far in solving the problems. Indeed, these graces help greatly, whatever the type of human beings one has to deal with !

" My experience, which, as you know, is a long one, has demonstrated to me that most

of my disasters have come through my losing
my temper ! In my younger days many were
the humiliations I suffered ! Perhaps I have
grown in grace a little and won a bit more
control over this vile ' ego.'

" We have been a month now in England.
To compensate for the lack of sunshine, we
have had to pile on more clothing. Dr.
Hooker sent me to Charing Cross Hospital,
where I was X-rayed and otherwise examined. The surgeon found a nasty internal
growth. Dr. Huggins also discovered it in
Rhodesia and told my wife about it but kept
the news from me.

" So now I know the disconcerting truth.
Being of the earth earthy, this gave me a shock.
But grace for the hour of need is ever forthcoming. The truths I have preached to others come
with comfort to my heart. I am sure God cannot be unkind. When I contemplate the whole
situation dismay lays hold of me. But I *do*
know this, that each day's need will be met.

" We have taken a house at Kingsmead
Close, Selly Oak, Birmingham, and there we
hope to go in June.

" Without doubt there are signs that a
revival of religion is close at hand. The
things that the Oxford Group stands for are
getting hold of Christian people.

" We hope you are, by now, glad parents !
Our love to you both."

This letter was the first that brought to
many friends in Southern Rhodesia the final
confirmation of the sad news that the disease,
which had all along been suspected, was
actually there, and had to be borne to the
end. Love and sympathy went out from all
hearts to Mrs. White as she was called upon
to face a sorrow and a suffering hardly less,
perhaps, than that of her dear husband.
Mary Smallwood, who had helped formerly
at Waddilove, came to Mrs. White's assistance at Kingsmead Close when the illness became more serious and continual nursing was
needed. Her help at such a time was invaluable,
as she had the strength and skill to move him
lightly and easily from side to side in his pain.
Her unselfish devotion never flagged.

John told me later on, that when the news
was first broken to him by the hospital
surgeon, and the first overwhelming shock
was over, a great longing had come into his
heart to return with Mrs. White to Mashonaland at once before it was too late, and to die
among his own people. More than once he
had actually made up his mind to do so, but
something kept him back and prevented him
from fulfilling his intention.

When we consider the wonderful ministry, especially among the young, that God gave him to carry through to the end from his bed of sickness in England, and the joy in Christ which he brought into the lives of others, we cannot doubt that he was being led along the right path, and that the inner voice which forbade him to return to Rhodesia was the voice of his Lord. God had a mighty work for John to do, which could only be accomplished in England.

Yet he would grow despondent at times and wonder whether he had really done the right thing in staying on. Many times over he reminded me of the promise which he had given, that he would die, if God thus willed it, among his own Mashona people.

Simon Chihota, in his own direct manner, shows us how strong the call had been from Africa and how deeply it had moved John White's heart.

" In our mind," Simon wrote, " Baba White is a great missionary and a good model Christian. His attitude towards us, his whole-hearted love for us, his willingness to assist us even in the smallest things—all these things are a sermon to us.

" More than once he has stood up for us against overwhelming odds, even staking his life for our people in 1896. No one has been more instrumental in bringing us the Word of God.

" There was a great shortage of food in the year 1922 and Baba White helped us. It was then he promised to die amongst us and that promise gladdened our hearts. A great number of the Mashona people came to know of it and believe it. We secretly selected a spot as a site for his grave at a place in our country where he did most of his good works.

" We pray that those who have the direction of things will be divinely guided to consider our view in this matter. Baba White is idolised amongst us. The African people say ' We do not want him to go away.'

" They appeal to everyone in power to help to keep Baba White in Rhodesia. We feel that his work is not finished amongst us. He knows us better than anyone else. We appeal to him that he should not leave us. We cannot be too emphatic on this point. We want him now and we want him always.

" I, Simon Chihota, have received many letters to this effect and I have been asked to write this letter."

It was hard indeed for John White to resist such a child-like appeal as this. He told me how greatly the matter had troubled him. He had made it for some time a subject for daily prayer for guidance, seeking the will of God.   At last he had become inwardly convinced that he ought to remain.   But he had decided at the same time that all that remained of his mortal body, after cremation, should be buried in a grave at a spot which the Mashona people had chosen, so that he might at least in this way fulfil his promise to them.

The next letter to Frank Mussell congratulates the happy parents on the birth of a son.

" In the last week's *Methodist Recorder*," he writes, " we read the joyful news that unto you a son has been born.   May God bless the wee chappie, and also those to whom he has been entrusted.   He must be a source of great joy to you both, as also to the Sisters. It will likewise be a proud experience for you to introduce him to your friends in England next year when you return on furlough . . .

" I seem to have gone down the hill quite a bit during the last ten days.   Two doctors gave me a minor operation a week ago and since then I have suffered a lot of pain.   So I abide somewhat in the shadows.   Where suffering is concerned, I am afraid I do not belong to the heroic type.   Yet I *do* know that what He wills is best, and this brief period in what we call Time is but a speck in God's Eternity.   If this weakness and

suffering makes me even in the faintest degree
fitter for the fellowship of the fuller life, then
it is to be welcomed.

" A man brought in an armful of books the
other day to choose therefrom. There were
a few of the useless type, but I dug out one
gem—Forbes Robinson's ' Letters to his
Friends.' He was a Don at Cambridge,
brilliant in all his subjects, who died before
he reached the age of forty. He had a soul
of beauty which he poured out in these noble
letters to his friends. The highest culture
combined with deep spirituality and wonderful insight into the things of God. It does
seem that some of the greatest saints have
not lived to a great age.

" I note that four American fundamentalists
have not been allowed to enter Rhodesia
because the Government considered that their
teaching was distracting the Africans. On
this question I have repeatedly fought the
Government and have contended that it is
not *their* function to say who shall, or who
shall not, preach the Gospel. To talk about
' disturbing the natives ' is bunkum. That
does not concern His Majesty's Ministers
when it pleases them to pass an Ordinance!
If it is as I saw it reported then this new
encroachment on our religious freedom ought

to be strenuously resisted. With the credentials He had, our Lord would never have got past Plumtree !¹   Well, old friend, I must stop. May the divine blessing be on you and your colleagues in all your attempts to give the good news to Africa."

Frank Mussell at this time felt strongly that it might be the will of God, in answer to faithful and earnest prayer, to restore John to health. Without any word of disparagement of modern surgery, Frank wrote to John about the miracles of healing which were evident signs of Christ's power in the Early Church. Could not the same power be witnessed in John to-day, for the glory of God, if only faith were strong enough ? He therefore had asked for the prayers of faithful men and women both in America and England, and had written to Pastor Jeffreys.

"Your letter," John writes in answer, "touched me very deeply, dear Comrade. It made me look at my own position with regard to faith-healing. One does vaguely think on these things without having a definite conviction.

"A few nights after your letter came, for one whole night I failed to get to sleep. For a long time I had very happy and intimate

¹ A frontier town.

fellowsl.ip with our Lord. I told Him what
was the extent of my faith in Him. Nothing
in heaven or earth could baffle His skill.
I remembered, in His presence, that so many
of His disciples were praying for me. Then
I said : ' Lord, if Thou wilt, Thou canst
make me whole ! '

" I am unable to get past that proviso.
Am I dishonouring Christ ? These good folk
in America, and the Pastor you mention in
England, are without doubt mighty in prayer.
I presume they don't put the case as I do.
They make no stipulation. There is a very
wonderful case reported by Hugh Redwood
in *God in the Shadows*. His daughter was
healed directly in answer to prayer.

" Well, dear Comrade, your letter has
cheered me greatly, and impressed me with
the possibilities of prayer. Mrs. White sent
on your letter to Dr. Dunning, at Cliff, and
asked them to join the company of be-
seechers. . . . I was reading the letters of
Forbes Robinson to his friends. His theory
was to concentrate on individuals and give
half an hour, an hour, or sometimes more, to
the need of one man. When one comes to
the end of life, one feels what a vastly more
impressive life one might have lived. I am
writing to the converted, I know, but how

carefully one should guard these sacred hours !
It is dangerously possible to spread one's
activities over the illimitable veld and get
nowhere. How intense our Lord was ! He
lived in the closest fellowship. . . . We both
trust that the baby and the babe's mother are
well. Our love to you."

The next letter is dated November 3rd,
1932. By this time the response had been
given, in God's own wonderful way, to the
faithful prayers that had been offered, and
a change was noticed by all. For a time
even the physical suffering had been greatly
relieved, but the greatest change had come
in the inner life. John himself realised this.
The gloom of depression which had over-
shadowed him during the earlier days of his
illness had now been dispersed, and a radiant
assurance shone out in his eyes and face
which bore its own message to those who
came to see him. It showed that his sorely
troubled spirit was now at rest.

Frank and his family came back to England
early in the year 1933. One last letter from
John reached them before they started.

" It cheered me," John wrote, " to get
your letter, dear Comrade, a few days ago.
What a fine friend you are, so full of real
sympathy and hope ! You dear people, in

your references to me, are altogether too appreciative. I am a very imperfect Christian, and keep on repeating to my Lord day by day :

Nothing in my hand I bring,
Simply to Thy Cross I cling.

But for the abounding mercy of God, I would not have kept on with this work. So let every bit of honour go to Him to whom it belongs !

" Sometimes the way does seem very long and very dreary. But in the sleepless nights I have my Divine Friend close beside me. I get weaker, which is natural. Anyhow, this experience has drawn me into deeper fellowship with God. That is worth much !

" Now, old friend, every Christian blessing to your wife and yourself. My love to the two Sisters. Please greet all my African friends, and say I remember and pray for them."

One further letter from John lies before me, written to Arthur Cripps at Enkeldoorn.

" Have you," he asks, " any theory on the utility of physical pain ? A lady friend of ours said that spiritual pain might bring us nearer to God, but she saw no use in physical pain. Lately, I have passed through some severe ordeals, and have thought much about its effect on me. It certainly gives me better to understand and sympathise with other sufferers. It also helps me to enter into fellowship with Him, whose body was beaten and pierced, and who passed away in physical agony. It also urges me to pray for those who are in distress. But sometimes the way does seem dark, and I have need to pray for faith to go forward."

The meaning of all this suffering which John bore so patiently was brought home to me in a letter that I received, after he had passed away, from a young medical student who had often gone into that upper room where John lay dying. He had shared with John some of his own difficulties of faith and had been wonderfully helped by what he saw and heard.

" Experience," he wrote to me, " of hospital life had implanted an ever-growing questioning in my mind. Was the Christianity, which I was just feeling in its first youthful glow, adequate for disease ? I was doing surgery, and many remarkable and rapid cures brought to me the wondrous joy of healing. Yet, in the background, was the grim problem of the incurables—the quiet, patient men and women, who came to us in simple trust for healing and were sent empty away.

" Was Christianity adequate for *this* ? They were so afraid, these simple people. Many

of them were terrified. Was it adequate
not merely for resignation, but for creative
acceptance ? That was what I wanted for
them ! Was it possible ?

" My experience of Christ, strong as it was,
had not yet been purified by the fire of
discipline sufficiently for me to answer that
question. And then John White came into
my life and answered my question.

" I understood the Master better through
contact with him, who was surely one of His
most honoured servants. One phrase of
Scripture which seemed to reach the very
core of my problem, was translated by what
I saw into vital flame :

" ' Who, for the joy that was set before
Him, endured the Cross, despising the shame.'

" In our Lord's presence, disease was not
grappled with in grim defiance : it was turned
into creative witness. Suffering was transmuted
into joy. Death was swallowed up in victory."

" Donald " was the name of this medical
student, and he used to bring others with
him, and ask if they also could share his
privilege of seeing John White. However
weak John might be, he would never allow
any young student to be turned away during
his long illness. Even if he could only speak
a few words, he would have them brought

upstairs and give them a word of good cheer in the Saviour's Name.

Who knows whether some one or other of those, whose hearts were thus touched with love for their Lord, may find their way to Southern Rhodesia, or elsewhere, as the years go on ?   Who knows if one of them may not be called to serve in the Hospital which we hope to dedicate to John's memory among the Mashona people whom he loved ?

" A few weeks ago," writes J. W. Stanlake, " I went to see John in Kingsmead Close, and our conversation turned towards the problems that confront the missionary to-day. " No man," said John, " can help these folk unless he loves them.   He must love them in order to save them."

This was in brief, the substance of all that John said to those who came to see him. Therefore if the flame of love which was in his own heart has kindled, as a flame will do, a corresponding love for Christ in the hearts of any one of those young folk who came to visit him, or who reads this story about him, then, Oh then ! may it not constrain them to follow John's example and help to complete the work which he had undertaken in Rhodesia ?

Arthur Cripps, when I was with him at Enkeldoorn, visiting the hospital, told me about one of the last of John's letters to him. In this letter, John had written about founding a hospital for the Mashona people somewhere near the centre of his own field of work. One of the objects of the book which I am now writing is to provide the nucleus of a fund to start such a hospital in John White's memory. The deeply touching appeal of Simon Chihota that their loved father and friend, Baba White, should never leave them, might find in this way one of its fulfilments. John's grave is in the midst of his own people. He has given that last gift to them. But surely, if the Church of Christ is a living Church, there should be a living memorial also in some young consecrated life of man or woman who would be ready to take up the work which he began and to love the people whom he loved.

If it were possible to build a Hospital and to provide it with devoted Christian workers, then the Mashona people would be able to realise that John White's remaining in England, during his last illness, had a purpose in it which God's Providence ordained, and that his sacred promise to them, that he would not leave them or forsake them, has not been broken.[1]

[1] If anyone who reads this story and is moved by this appeal desires to contribute a gift to the Hospital, or to write about personal service, a letter should be addressed to the Secretary, Methodist Missionary Society, 24, Bishopsgate, London, E.C.2, England.

CHAPTER XXIII : " I WILL FEAR NO EVIL "

THE actual date when I came to Selly Oak, Birmingham, and met John White for the first time at Kingsmead Close, was Christmas, 1932.

A College Fellowship had been generously offered me by the Council at Woodbrooke, in order that I might deliver a series of lectures in the College, and also find time to write a book.[1] The thought of being near to Dr. Rendel Harris, whom I deeply revered, made me eagerly accept the offer

But I had no idea at the time that John White of Mashonaland was lying ill in Kingsmead Close. If I had known it, my eagerness to go there would have been more than doubled. But God had this wonderful gift in store for me, and everything happened according to His will.

The book I was writing had proved much more difficult than any that I had yet attempted, and all through the previous summer and autumn I had struggled with it. It was intended to tell, as far as it could be

[1] *Christ in the Silence.*

told, from living personal experience, the
inner secret of Christ's presence, and I had
prayed to God to guide my steps into the
way of peace, so that the book might bring
peace to others. And He guided my steps
in His own way to that inner sanctuary, where
I met John White at Kingsmead Close and
found the peace that I needed. "How
unsearchable are his judgments and His ways
past finding out ! " [1]

Only once before had there been a slight
chance of my meeting John White—when I
was living at the Indian Students' Hostel, in
London—but it had fallen through. We had
known each other, however, by name for a
long time past, and we had a dear mutual
friend in Arthur Shearly Cripps. The great
struggle, which John and Arthur had been
carrying on so bravely in Southern Rhodesia,
year after year, was familiar to me, and it
had always filled me with deep admiration ;
for I had already twice visited that country,
and understood how serious were the
obstacles against which they were contending.

Mrs. Menon, a Danish lady who had
married an Indian Christian, Dr. Menon, was
living at 1, Kingsmead Close. They had two
little children, Nanie and Tangai, and I was

[1] Rom. ii. 33.

an old friend of the family.   It happened that
they had asked me to stay with them for a
few days till the College opened.   In this
way I learnt, on Christmas morning itself,
that John White of Mashonaland was lying
ill next door.   At once, in eager haste, I went
to meet him, and in that simple manner we
came to know and love one another on Christmas Day itself !   What a Christmas gift that
was !

It is not at all easy to describe in words
what that meeting meant to me, and how the
whole burden that I was then carrying
seemed to be lifted in a moment.   For I knew
that the answer had come to my earnest
prayers, and that in that dear sanctuary of
love and joy and peace the vivid consciousness of Christ's presence would be renewed
in my own life, and would flow into the book
that I was writing.,   For John—from the first
we began, quite naturally, to call each other
by our Christian names—soon became as
eager and intent on what I was writing as I
was myself.   He saw that it was the one great
longing of my heart to help the young leaders
of the new generation to carry forward the
glorious service of Christ in the wide world,
which had meant all in all to us.   This was
his longing also, and so he sought to help me

in every way he could. We prayed together
every morning and evening that what I wrote
might be used, in God's love, for the glory
of His name and the work of His Kingdom.

"Each day," I wrote in the Preface to
my book, "we have prayed together : and
this book has been the constant subject of
our prayers. To be with John White, in
such times of heart-outpouring to God in
prayer, has been for me a benediction. The
sense of the nearness of Christ's presence has
been with me as I have gone to and fro, seeing
him each day. With deepest gratitude and
affection I am dedicating this book to him."
These words I chose after many attempts to
write down exactly what God's gift of John
White had been to me.

Christ has said, that where two or three
are gathered together in His name, He is in
the midst. It was His presence which we
found, as we gave our hearts in prayer to Him
with our one great object in view.

Since that day, when we thus wrote
together (for though the words were mine,
the spirit was his, if there is any need to speak
of distinctions when the unity was so complete), letters have come which have shown,
without a question, that what we prayed for
has come to pass.

I have already mentioned how, during
that closing year of his life, John's thoughts
seemed always directed towards the young.[1]
Nothing in the world gave him a greater joy
than when some young Christian, who was
starting the battle of life, as a good soldier
of Jesus Christ, would come to see him.

"Lad," he would say, with glowing eyes,
" I'm glad to see you ! "

And before they had parted, the boy's head
would be bowed low at John's bedside as he
dedicated his whole life anew to his Saviour
in prayer, and a benediction would follow
while the eyes of both would be filled with
tears.

It may be that I have dwelt at too great
length upon the symbol of this book which
seemed to bind us like a sacrament together,
but thus it came about, and I wished to tell
the story quite simply.

Every day my heart was drawn more and
more towards him as he lay there : for his
brave and tender spirit shone out in his eyes,
and his love for the Master was betokened
in every word he uttered. How I loved to
hear him read, when he was well enough, the
portion of the Word which he had chosen
for our daily devotion ! The Bible was the

[1] See p. 283.

one " Book of Life " to him, and he almost knew the New Testament by heart.

It seemed to me that, as his days on earth became fewer in number, and he knew the end was approaching, he went back to St. John's Gospel and Epistles most of all for his daily reading ; and he was profoundly interested when I searched the records of different Christian lives in order to find how far this was true of others.[1]

Jack Hoyland, who had been out with me in India and has himself the heart of a child, became very dear to John, and helped him much in times of bodily weakness when the spirit needed human comfort. If it was necessary for me to be away in London, it was always understood between us that Jack should come instead of me for a quiet time of prayer before the evening drew to its close.

Another dear friend, who had been an old and much-loved companion of John, was Victor Murray, who was teaching at this time in the Selly Oak College. The two old friends used to remain together side by side, often in quiet stillness, while thoughts that could not be uttered passed between them. Victor Murray and his wife were themselves very soon to enter the valley of the shadow, when

[1] See *Christ in the Silence*, pp. 105 and 314.

their daughter died quite suddenly who was the light of their home, and deeply loved by John himself.

In the household at Kingsmead Close we soon became a family of brothers and sisters. Mrs. White and Mary Smallwood won admiration from every one who saw them for their utterly devoted nursing, carried on without a single break. Night and day alike they never tired.

We would make the arrangement, with laughter behind it, that I was not to appear in the morning until the room was tidied up and all the washing was over and John's hair was brushed and he was " at his best." The fun went on with the pretence that John, like a good South African, enjoyed his cup of tea at eleven o'clock. So at eleven I would duly appear and we would have our tea together, though his cup would often remain untouched.

At Easter and Whitsuntide we all shared with him the Sacrament at his bedside and remembered how when the doors were shut in that upper room, in Jerusalem, our Lord had instituted for all time the Memorial of His Passion. These were the most sacred moments of all and they can never be forgotten. At the Easter Festival, he was well enough to conduct the service himself ; but at Whitsuntide, he was much weaker and requested me to take the service for him.

At other times, those who had been with him in the Mission Field, or in the home Church, came and ministered to him. He was able with his own hand to baptise Frank Mussell's two youngest children, and the times of sacred fellowship they had together cheered him more than words can tell. Dr. Lofthouse and Dr. Howard came over from Handsworth College whenever it was possible to do so.

One trait in John's character came out with singular beauty during these last days— his love for little children. Friends whom I met in Southern Rhodesia have told me that this was always one of the most marked features in his sunny nature, and I can well believe it from what I saw at Kingsmead Close.

Next door to him were Mrs. Menon's two little girls whom he greatly loved to have with him whenever he was free from pain. They were learning to play the piano and sometimes the sound would come through to his room, but he would never have it stopped if he could possibly help it. When the children very gently came up to his room to

show him something they had made, or to
bring him their dolls, he would make a great
fuss about it and be filled with admiration as
they told him all their wonderful secrets.
They would creep up the stairs on tip-toe and
peep in at the door to see if he was awake.   In
the spring and summer weather he would
watch them at play in the garden and wave
his hand to them from the window, and they
would wave back to him time after time.
Other children came to the garden and he
knew them all by name.

There was one other, of quite a different
age, whom he loved to have with him.   We
called her " Grannie."   Formerly she had come
to Mrs. Menon's house to help occasionally in
the house work.   Then she was taken very
ill.   She had suffered from the same illness
as John and had gone through a major
operation.   It was a great pleasure to John
to see her, when she went to spend the day
at Mrs. Menon's house after her illness, and
it was a joy to him to hear her speak of her
own deep love for her Saviour who had helped
her, night and day, through her illness.

" Now, Grannie," John would say, " you
must pray for me to-night that Jesus may be
with me all through the night."   John's
sister and niece and other dear relations

cheered him constantly by their frequent
visits. He was never lonely during those last
months.

The nights were often sleepless and not
seldom fraught with pain, but his Divine
Companion took away much of the long trial
of them and made their weariness less hard
to bear. No one could have been more
patient than he was, and his tenderness
towards every living creature on God's earth
seemed to increase daily. The early days
on the farm at Stainburn, in Cumberland,
were often brought back to his vivid imagination, and every animal and bird and flower
and tree seemed to bring to him its own
message of God's infinite fatherly love.

The month of April, in 1933, was marked
out by the radiant glory of the spring flowers
and the bright days of sunshine, after a dull
and gloomy winter. A very precious gift
of an invalid's bed, which could be moved
easily about the room, had been made to
John just at the beginning of this perfect
spring weather. It was his constant delight
to have his bed wheeled close up to the
window where he could see the blossom
beginning to open out on the fruit trees and
could watch the unfolding of the new leaves.

He would recall, with wistful eyes, the days

of spring in his old home at the farm. " It's spring-time in Cumberland now," he would say, " and the fields are all yellow with buttercups."

That Easter Sunday, in 1933, was a day of peculiar loveliness. The daffodils were plentiful that year. Masses of them were growing in the garden outside John's window and others were standing mingled with hyacinth and narcissus round his room. It was indeed a Day of Resurrection. The glory of the outer world seemed to prophesy a new beginning, if only Christ could be born anew in the hearts of men.

Spring had nearly passed with all its fresh beauty when Whitsuntide drew near. That special year, 1933, I had been asked long beforehand, to take part in a young people's Whitsuntide Camp, which was being held not far away at Harborne, with the Methodist Church as its centre. A quaint anagram, " Whych," had been devised as the abbreviation of the undertaking, meaning Whitsun Holiday Youth Camp, Harborne. The young members of all the Churches were uniting in prayer for an outpouring of the Holy Spirit, as on the first Day of Pentecost.

Everything was being ordered and arranged by the young members themselves. They

were meeting on the Friday evening before
Whit-Sunday and were continuing their " re-
treat " until the evening of Whit-Monday.
Their constant prayer was that they might
receive power from on high, so that, in
Christ's name, they might become witnesses,
not merely in England and Scotland, but
" unto the uttermost parts of the earth." [1]

Many of those who were prayerfully sharing
together in this adventure of faith had already
surrendered their lives to Christ through
coming into touch with the Oxford Group
Movement. Some of these became natural
leaders at a time when leadership was most
needed. Others were hoping to go out as
missionaries to distant lands in the years
to come. Many had come in for the week-
end from distant parts of England and all
were expecting a blessing. The whole movement had been " begun, continued and
ended " in prayer and childlike trust in God's
power to bless more abundantly than we
could either ask or think.

John's whole heart went out in love and
sympathy towards these young men and
women in their earnestness and devotion of
spirit and in their silent waiting upon God in
prayer for a revival of the gift of the Holy Spirit.

[1] Acts i. 8.

Those Whitsuntide days seemed to lift him up almost beyond the reach of pain as he became absorbed in this movement among the young people in the home-land, which might bring blessing to the larger mission field. It would seem as if he was renewing his own youth in the lives of others. The days were full of sunshine in the outer world and there was sunshine in his heart.

Those who went out from Woodbrooke to take part in these gatherings at Harborne went first into that sanctuary of prayer, in the upper room where John was lying, and he would pour out his soul in blessing on them for their work in Christ's name. What a strength he gave us, no words of mine can express! We went from him direct to these devotional meetings and we took his spirit with us.

A hush came upon all the young men and women assembled in the Methodist Church as I told them something of the story of this heroic servant of God who in his illness was praying for them. I also told them what that upper room in Kingsmead Close had meant to me and to many others also. They sent him back a message of love.

Many lives were changed at these gatherings and hearts were completely surrendered to Christ by the power of the Holy Spirit.

A still wider movement seems likely to grow out of those times of pentecostal blessing at Harborne in 1933, and larger circles may be reached. In the Whitsuntide of 1934 great things were again expected and great things were accomplished. The medical student, from whose touching letter I quoted in an earlier chapter, has been one of the main supporters and helpers in this wonderful endeavour to bring back in spirit, in our own times, the first days of the Christian Church.

During the present year, 1935, a still more earnest effort is to be made and if the way is open for me, they have asked me once more to be among them. Since that gathering at Harborne in 1933 owed so much to John's inspiration, I would ask for the prayers of those who read this book that this present year and the years to come may see the movement grow in depth of spiritual life as well as in the width of its appeal.

CHAPTER XXIV : THOU ART WITH ME

THESE sacred days with John White at Kingsmead Close were now drawing to an end. A further examination by the London specialist had conclusively proved that no major operation was possible, and though John never doubted for a moment his Lord's power to heal even the worst disease, it became clear to him that the time of his departure was at hand.

He often spoke about this to me and loved to have me read over the perfect music of the old version in 2 Corinthians, where St. Paul writes :

" For which cause we faint not : but though our outward man perish, yet the inward man is renewed day by day.

" For our light affliction, which is but for a moment, worketh for us a far more exceeding and eternal weight of glory ;

" While we look, not at the things which are seen, but at the things which are not seen.

" For the things which are seen are

THOU ART WITH ME

temporal : but the things that are not seen are eternal.''[1]

Great and glorious words of comfort such as these became filled with a new meaning for both of us, while John looked death steadily in the face. He never shrank from it. Rather, he silently longed for it, with an intense desire, if only the Master would but give the one word of release, which would set him free.

The story must now be told—for it is typical of John's humility—how I was able at last to overcome his extremely sensitive shyness and dedicate the volume to him which had been the fruit of so many of our prayers. From the very first I had determined to do so. Only one thing made me hesitate. I was almost desperately afraid of a refusal ! His own modesty was so intense, that again and again when I was on the point of broaching the subject I hesitated lest he should raise some final objection.

Then a morning came when he was visibly sinking. Indeed, when I went to him at the usual hour he was too ill even to take his own part in our morning prayer together. He said, " Charlie, you pray this morning." At the end of my own prayer he said the Benediction in a very low voice and we parted.

[1] 2 Cor. iv. 16 to end.

That day it was absolutely necessary for me to go up to London, and I did so with much misgiving. But I was returning the same evening. So ill was John, that all the way to the station the thought began to haunt me that he might even pass away before I came back—he seemed so very weak. But I could not bear the thought that he should not know about the dedication of my book to him. So I sent him from the railway station a long telegram, telling him what a joy it would be to me if he would allow me to dedicate my book to him.

As it happened John rallied through the day instead of getting worse, and when I returned in the evening and went up to see him the pain had decreased.

He greeted me with the deepest affection, but there was a somewhat troubled look in his eyes, as if he had something on his mind that he wanted to get rid of.

" Charlie," he said to me, " I got your telegram, but you mustn't *think* of dedicating your book to me ! There are many other people, who are your friends, far better known than I am ; and I am quite unworthy of it ! "

" No, John ! " I said to him quickly, " There's only you, John : and I've made up

my mind once for all! For you've helped
me more than anyone else in the world, and
the book belongs, by right, to you. It's
yours, John, just as much as it is mine."

He could see the truth of what I said
shining in my eyes, and understood that it
was not a mere passing wish to give him
pleasure in his illness. So he accepted and
we had our evening prayer together.

After this had been finally settled between
us he would try to read over, very carefully, in its draft form, each chapter as soon
as I had finished it. Sometimes he would
be too unwell to do so, but most of the book
went through his hands and his criticism was
always most helpful. The feeling, that he
was really helping me, buoyed him up and
certainly gave him great comfort.

It was a very great joy to us all that the
book was actually published in time for him
to be able to keep the volume by his side and
read it in quiet moments. He was able also
to send it to his friends Arthur Cripps and
Frank Mussell and others both in England
and Southern Rhodesia.

During the latter portion of July, 1933, the
sudden summons came to me to go back to
India. More and more the inner voice seemed
to tell me not to delay. At length it was so

unmistakably clear that it was necessary to break the news to John.

This was the hardest thing I had to face while making up my mind to depart : for John had drawn so close to me in the bonds of Christian love and fellowship that I could hardly bear to think of the pain it would bring him, in his extreme weakness, when I came to say good-bye.

But I found that he had already anticipated what must ultimately happen ; and instead of holding me back by any entreaty, he pressed me earnestly not to think of him for a moment, but rather to go forward to the work in India that God was calling me to perform.

That night, after making the decision, we had our prayer together. John prayed that the long sea journey I was about to take might be guided by God aright, and might come to a successful issue.. His prayer was wonderfully answered.

On the Sunday before my departure we partook of the Sacrament together in that upper room. We knew that it was, in very truth, the Last Supper of the Lord which we should receive in union together here on earth.

Just before sailing I returned from London to snatch a few moments with John. Then we prayed our last united prayer in that

sanctuary where I had knelt so often at his
bedside. Christ's presence was with us, and
John kept his brightness radiantly until I had
departed.

Later on when his wife entered the room
she found him silently weeping.

All through that voyage to the East I had
a constant sense of his companionship. So
close was it that I found myself continually
writing letters to him. These accumulated in
my drawer until I posted them at the next
port of call. He never received those letters ;
but they gave great comfort to his wife in
the first days of her bereavement.

One simple record of a conversation which
I had with John before we parted must be
told over again. For it best reveals the
depth of his character and his fervent love
for his Lord.[1]

One evening, I had read over to him some
portions of a new chapter which I had drafted
on the words of Christ, " I am the True Vine."
After it was over, John had gone on to recall
the verse which follows in the Gospel story
about the " greater love," when a man lays
down his life for his friends. Then I left
him for the night with a great peace in my
heart.

[1] I have told it in *Christ in the Silence,* but it will bear repeating.

In the morning his face was radiant with an indescribable inner joy, and he greeted me with the words, "Only think of it, Charlie! He has called us friends! No longer servants, but friends! If He had called us servants, it would have been more than we deserved. But He has called us friends!

"Last night, when I could not sleep, that wonderful thought came to me, and the joy seemed to overcome all the pain. For I saw how it was through this very suffering that He was drawing me nearer to Himself—through the Cross. For only the *friend* can know what the Lord Himself suffered."

His voice broke in tears as he spoke of our Lord's suffering on the Cross. "You mustn't mind," he said, "my being sentimental. It's just the weakness that comes over me owing to this sickness."

"Yes," he went on, "I've learnt more about the love of God during this illness than I had ever known before. If I were asked whether I would live over this last year again, with all its suffering, I would not hesitate for a moment. It has been such a lesson to me! I thought I knew God in Africa, out on the lonely veld, and in the times of great danger—and so I did. For

He has been with me all these years. But
this sickness has brought me a new experience
of His love. He has been my Friend! That
makes all the difference!"

He would continually return to this theme
of God's love; and it seemed as if he were
never tired of dwelling upon it. That was
the divine mystery—God's love for him, a
sinner. "Who loved *me*, and gave Himself
for *me*." It started from the very depths
and soared up into the heights.

John never for a moment forgot those
depths, out of which he had been drawn
upward by God's grace. He never presumed
on God's mercy. He was the humblest of
men, knowing that in him, John White,
dwelt no good thing apart from God. He
had been taken "out of the bottomless pit,
out of the mire and clay," and his feet had
been set upon a Rock. This had been God's
doing, and it was marvellous in his eyes.

But now all this grace and mercy of forgiveness had been turned into Love itself—the
perfect Love that casts out fear! That was
the marvellous difference!

No verses in the Old Testament were
dearer to him than the opening words of the
fifty-third chapter of Isaiah. When the
choice was given to me during his illness, I

would constantly turn to these ; and he
would repeat the words over and over again,
which he knew by heart. " All we like sheep
have gone astray. We have turned everyone
to his own way. And the Lord hath laid on
Him the iniquity of us all."

Once I told him the story of a poor woman
in Sunderland, who could not find her release
from the crushing burden of sin which
weighed her down. Good Friday had come,
and I had asked her the simple question,
" Can you doubt for a moment that when
Jesus, your Lord and Master, uttered those
great words upon the Cross, ' It is finished,'
He did not mean what He said. He brought
to an end your sins and mine."

That simple statement, spoken in His
name, had brought release. The burden of
her sins was laid down at the foot of the Cross.

When I went on to tell John of the light
that shone in her eyes and the joy that came
into her life, he spoke to me about his own
conversion in the old Methodist church, at
Stainburn, fifty years ago ; how in the glow
of that first love for his Lord, he used to
wander among the Cumberland mountains,
and all the hills and valleys would seem to
shout and laugh for joy, as they echoed his
songs of praise to Christ, his Saviour and

Redeemer. So great was that flood-burst of his heart's devotion that it could not be contained within bounds.

All through those fifty years—he told me very humbly—Christ had been his Good Shepherd, leading him beside green pastures and still waters and restoring his soul. And now, as the valley of the shadow of death was entered, he feared no evil; for his Good Shepherd was with him. His rod and His staff gave him comfort. While he lay there, with his outward strength failing, his inward strength was being renewed day by day; and something of the joy of that first love for Christ had come back into his life, filling his heart each day with sunshine and gladness.

When I had said good-bye to him on the day before I left for India it was clear to me that the end was very near at hand. As it happened, in God's providence, it came suddenly within three days of my departure.

The pain became so great at the last (so I was told by those who were with him) that he sank into a comatose state and had only rare moments of recognition. He was hardly able to speak, but made a sign that the prayers offered for him had given him comfort. Once he raised his hand and pointed as if something had been made clear to his inner vision, but he sank back again without a word.

During one of the last times of full consciousness, Jack Hoyland, whom he loved very dearly indeed, told him of a destitute family he had just visited. John immediately made a sign to his wife and gave a gift of money for them.

Thus, even in his last moments, he was thinking of others rather than himself. This was almost his final conscious act, and it seemed to sum up the whole of his devoted love for Christ, his Lord, whose presence he had found among the least and the poorest of His brethren.

Even though he could not speak, he understood that loving prayers were being offered for him as he breathed his last. His tortured body was at rest.

Far away, out in Mashonaland, the news travelled across the air that John White had passed away and thousands who called him Father mourned his loss.

Baba was dead. The word went round all the villages and the grief was universal. All that he had done for them, how he had helped them in the great Famine, how he had healed their sick, how he had taken the same food

as they did and lived with them in their
own kraals, how he had brought to them in
their own tongue the Word of Life, how he
had died in a far-off land, but had asked to
be buried among them—all these things were
recalled about him, and in the generations to
come the same stories will be treasured about
his goodness and it will be said, " He was a
man of God : he loved us as his own children.
He was a Father to us all."

" Greater love," the Master has said, " hath
no man than this, that a man lay down his
life for his friends."

" Ye are my friends, if ye do whatsoever I
command you.

" These things I command you that ye
love one another."

That " greater love " John White had
shown to those whom Christ had called him
to serve ; and among the Mashona people
his name will never be forgotten.

CHAPTER XXV : THE LIVING CHRIST

CHRIST comes to us, as the Lord of Life, in this our own generation, at the dawn of a new era in the world's history. Mighty events have been happening before our eyes, such as probably no other generation in the annals of mankind has witnessed. Every continent has been shaken with upheaval, as if an earthquake had suddenly burst through the thin crust of human civilisation and the molten lava were cutting its own new channels through the soil. Africa, most recent of all in its rude awakening, has been convulsed by one shock after another, as gold, diamond, and copper have been discovered, which modern machinery has been able to extract at a tremendous cost in human lives.

The New Age has begun. Christ again stands on the shore, at its dawn, and bids us cast out our nets on the right side of the ship. We obey, and by the very act of obedience realise afresh His power and His love.

Mystical truths such as these, which we rightly read into the Gospel story, find their own interpretation for us when we look back over the long life of John White so bravely and heroically lived among the Mashona people. For in significant ways, by many of his actions and ideas, he was far ahead of his times. He was a pioneer of this New Age. Only later, when Mashona History is written, will what he did be recognised in all its greatness.

" The testimony of Jesus,"[1] says the writer of Revelation, " is the Spirit of Prophecy." John had that testimony deep within him from the time when in his first love for Christ he went brooding among the Cumberland Hills. His life was in tune with what Shakespeare has so finely called

> *. . . the soul of the wide world,*
> *Dreaming of things to come.*

In God's mercy and loving-kindness he had been given, while still a lad, on his father's farm at Stainburn, the inestimable grace of inward conversion to Christ, his Saviour and his Lord. This grace had never left him, but was always there, in his heart, as " a well of water springing up unto everlasting life."[2]

As he grew older, he had the further grace given to him, by the one and selfsame Spirit,

[1] Rev. xix. 10. [2] John iv. 14.

of not looking inwardly too often at his own
soul's growth, but of being able to lose his
life for others, as he went out in the larger
life of Christ and His Church among the
Mashona people. With the Apostle Paul, he
became an ambassador for Christ on their
behalf, as though God did beseech them by
him. He "prayed for them, in Christ's
stead, that they would be reconciled to God."[1]

This ministry of grace to the Mashona people
he was conscious of, as being committed to
him by God Himself, and he could in no wise
leave it on one side. He had been called and
chosen to be an apostle of the Mashona people :
he was a debtor to them ; and still further
(as we have seen) he had desired to die among
them. In true response, his African converts
were loyal to him with a touching fidelity
and affection. He became Baba, Father, to
them—their Father in God—consecrated
with an ordination " not of men, nor by man,
but by Jesus Christ and God the Father who
had raised Christ from the dead."[2]

Thus he was able to realise, in true per-
spective and with far-seeing eyes, how new
things as well as old must be brought out of
the treasury of God on their behalf, if he
would be to them in very truth " a scribe

[1] 2 Cor. v. 20.   [2] Gal. i., 1.

instructed unto the Kingdom of Heaven."
He had the confidence that Jesus, his Lord
and Master, had bidden him go forward
along untrodden ways. He followed and
obeyed.

Those first days, when he came up to live
among the Mashona, forty years ago, were
unique. Such a new birth in the history of
a people can never happen twice. He had
witnessed—as if arising out of the pangs of
suffering and martyrdom which followed the
rebellion—the actual birth of the Mashona
nation ; not the old pagan race of timid,
cowering, hunted men and women, sunk so
low in superstition as to appear almost un-
redeemable in their degradation, but a
spiritual house, a holy priesthood,[1] presented
unto Christ, sanctified and cleansed—" a
glorious Church, not having spot or wrinkle
or any such thing, but holy and without
blemish."[2]

If these words, taken from the apostolic
writings of the first age of the Church, seem
to strike too high a note for such a theme as
the young Mashona Church in Southern
Rhodesia which we know to-day, we must
remember the gross sins that made both
Ephesus and Corinth a byword of shame

[1] Peter ii. 5. [2] Eph. v. 27.

and reproach in the ancient Græco-Roman world. Yet it is concerning the inhabitants of these very cities, after they had become Christians, that St. Paul could write :

" But ye are washed. But ye are sanctified. But ye are justified, in the name of the Lord Jesus Christ and by the Spirit of our God."[1]

Even so could John White exclaim as he rejoiced in the great change which had come into the lives of his own African converts. For God's grace is " mighty to the casting down of the strongholds of Satan," not merely in olden days in Asia Minor and Greece, but in our own days in Mashonaland as well.

At that remarkable period when John first reached the field of his labours, human life had become fluid once more. Mankind was " on trek." A whole sub-continent was suddenly beginning to shape itself afresh in new moulds, taking on new plastic forms.

To lose such a priceless opportunity, through lack of a larger vision, would have been to throw away the great gifts of love and sacrifice stored up in the hearts of the Mashona people instead of bringing them into the treasure-house of God's kingdom.

[1] Cor. vi., 11

John boldy seized the occasion with both hands and blazed a new trail for future missionary work. By so doing, he helped to keep the Mashona race from sinking back into degradation and serfdom when all was hanging in the balance.

I have seen, with sad eyes, the tragic consequence, when such an opportunity was lost long ago, farther south, in the Transvaal and other provinces of South Africa. I have seen Bantu tribes torn up from the soil and set to labour in the dark mines beneath the earth and then cast aside to carry new evils back to their own kraals. I have watched this traffic in the souls of men,[1] which was the last and worst sin of Babylon, being repeated in our own generation. And if things are not so inhumanly base to-day as they were when I first saw them in pre-War days, it is because men like John White and women also have " loved not their lives unto the death," and have testified against it.

Such heroes and heroines of the Faith, who cherish the larger vision, are bound to be persecuted and misunderstood by the world around them. For they have taken their place in the ranks of that army of the Living God, among those of every age, who

[1] Rev. xviii. 13.

Through faith subdued kingdoms,
Wrought righteousness, obtained promises,
Stopped the mouths of lions,
Quenched the violence of fire,
Escaped the edge of the sword,
Out of weakness were made strong,
Waxed valiant in fight,
Put to flight the armies of the aliens.
Women received their dead to life again,
And others were tortured,
Not accepting deliverance
That they might obtain a better resurrection.

No one would have rejoiced more than John to be counted worthy to suffer in that vanguard of the children of faith, which dies, but is never defeated. His whole nature, disciplined and schooled, tempered and chastened, by God's grace, was of the heroic type—" of whom the world was not worthy."

And the most noble thing about the whole story is this, that the Mashona people, whom he loved so dearly, *understood* him, not merely as a true and devoted friend who would do anything in his power to help them, but also as a true apostle of Jesus Christ who would recklessly hazard his life for Christ's sake and was prepared to abandon all in the service of his Lord and Master. This faith in

Christ, who was all in all to John White, had been realised afresh in a living manner by the first martyrs of the Mashona Church, James Anta, John Molele and many others, who had been ready to follow where John had led the way. For their heroism and devotion in times of persecution had reached the highest standard of Christian fortitude and endurance. Out of the midst of these persecutions, which had sifted the first Mashona disciples like wheat, there had been born a truly Christian Church. The Mashona followers of Jesus had gone forward, rejoicing that they were counted worthy to suffer for His Name."[1]

This volume that I have written will have shown again and again how true to their spiritual father in the faith these Mashona Christians were, and how, inspired by John's example, they went joyfully along the same road of love and sacrifice which he pursued. This is how I have read the story ; and that hallowed sanctuary of the dead at Waddilove, where all lie side by side together, is to me a sacrament of the one all-embracing love of Christ, whose length and breadth and depth and height surpass all human knowledge.

My last words in this book shall be to that

[1] Acts v. 41.

Mashona Church itself, as it keeps John White in remembrance. I would venture to speak in his name and with the blessing of the One Master whom we serve :

"Christ says to you, Mashona people, 'Fear not, little flock, for it is your Father's good pleasure to give you the Kingdom!' He has loved you with an everlasting love! He will never leave you nor forsake you! He will be with you, all the days, even to the end of the world!"

THE END

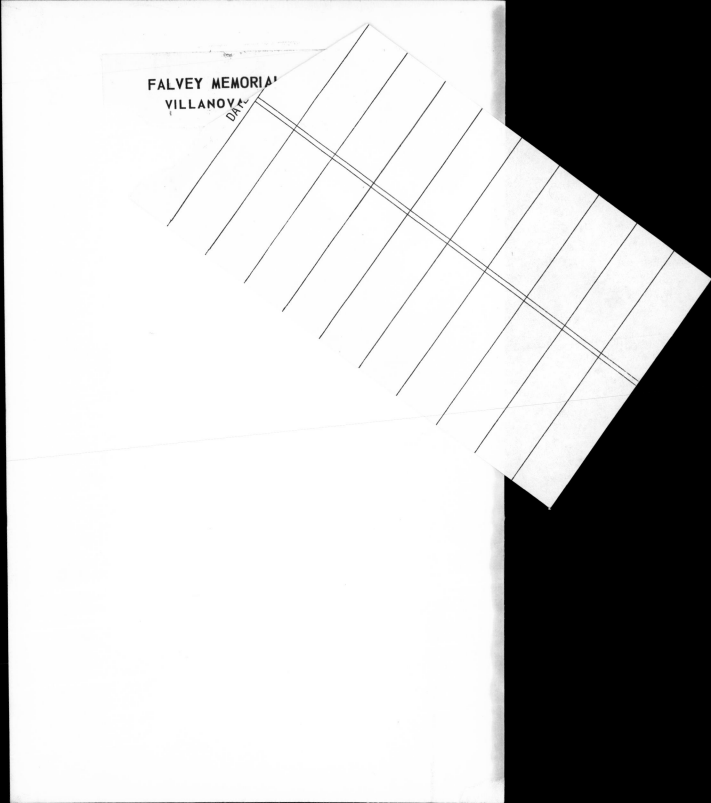